William Burnet Wright

Ancient Cities from the Dawn to the Daylight

William Burnet Wright

Ancient Cities from the Dawn to the Daylight

ISBN/EAN: 9783337117511

Printed in Europe, USA, Canada, Australia, Japan

Cover: Foto ©Lupo / pixelio.de

More available books at **www.hansebooks.com**

FROM THE DAWN TO THE DAYLIGHT

BY

WILLIAM BURNET WRIGHT

PASTOR OF THE BERKELEY STREET CHURCH, BOSTON

BOSTON AND NEW YORK
HOUGHTON, MIFFLIN AND COMPANY
The Riverside Press, Cambridge
1899

Copyright, 1886,
By WILLIAM BURNET WRIGHT.

All rights reserved.

EIGHTH IMPRESSION.

The Riverside Press, Cambridge, Mass., *U. S. A.*
Electrotyped and Printed by H. O. Houghton & Company.

TO THE MEMORY OF

HER

IN WHOSE SICK-CHAMBER, THE BEULAH OF HER HOUSEHOLD,

THESE STORIES OF THE PAST WERE TOLD,

AND BUT FOR WHOSE REQUEST THEY WOULD NOT HAVE BEEN PRINTED,

NOR EVEN WRITTEN DOWN,

They are Dedicated

BY

HER HUSBAND.

Now I saw in my dream, that by this time the Pilgrims were got over the Enchanted Ground, and entering into the country of Beulah, *whose air was very sweet and pleasant, the way lying directly through it, they solaced themselves there for a season. Yea, here they heard continually the singing of birds, and saw every day the flowers appear in the earth, and heard the voice of the turtle in the land. In this country the sun shineth night and day; wherefore this was beyond the Valley of the Shadow of Death, and also out of the reach of Giant Despair, neither could they from this place so much as see Doubting Castle. Here they were within sight of the city they were going to, also here met them some of the inhabitants thereof; for in this land the Shining Ones commonly walked, because it was upon the borders of heaven.*

PILGRIM'S PROGRESS.

PREFACE.

THIS little volume does not assume to be a learned work. If it were offered as a guide-book or a manual it would be an attempt of the blind to lead, and only the blind would follow. I am well aware that my knowledge of both archæology and history is far too slight to qualify me as an instructor in either. Of these subjects I know only so much as is familiar to all my ministerial brethren and probably less than is known to most of them. The purpose I have cherished is a humble one; so much so that even my ignorance may, perhaps, have been more of a help than a hindrance towards its accomplishment. For I have simply tried to imitate the child who peers through an opened door, and charmed by a glimpse of the wonders within the garden calls others to come and see. I have neither hoped nor endeavored to do more than awaken in those whose attention has not been turned toward the subjects brought before them in these pages an interest which may move them to seek ampler information from those who are competent to give it.

Where my authorities are at variance, the brevity of my sketches has compelled me simply to adopt the conclusions which seem to me correct, without pausing to discuss or even to repeat the views of those who hold different opinions.

The cities in which I have tried to interest the reader were so connected with the experiences of the chosen people that an acquaintance with any one of them can scarcely fail of throwing light upon some portion of the Bible. Each city, as the reader will perceive, has also been selected either because its history appears to illustrate pointedly some utterance of Christ, or because the manner in which it aided in preparing for the " New Jerusalem " is obvious.

In each sketch I have tried to indicate, as distinctly as I could, the character of the man or men for whose influence the name of the city stands. But when we think of the " New Jerusalem," all that draws our hearts toward it centres in Him who has laid its foundations and is still raising its walls. For this reason the concluding paper, which speaks of the " City which hath foundations," is longer than the others, and is given in two parts, of which the first is designed to show the working, the second to unveil the person, of its " Maker and Builder."

I am sincerely grateful to Professors E. C. Smyth, J. P. Taylor, and E. G. Coy, of Andover, and to the Rev. Lysander Dickerman, of Boston, for permitting me to read for their criticisms the proof-sheets of those papers which treat of subjects embraced in their respective departments of History, Assyriology, Greek, and Egyptology. Without indorsing my opinions, or becoming in the least responsible for any blunders of mine, which, in a review so rapid, may easily have escaped even their notice, these gentlemen have not discouraged me from publishing this little book.

BERKELEY STREET CHURCH,
July, 1886.

CONTENTS.

		PAGE
I.	Ur, the City of Saints	1
II.	Nineveh, the City of Soldiers	18
III.	Babylon, the City of Sensualists	35
IV.	Memphis, the City of the Dead	56
V.	Alexandria, the City of the Creed Makers	75
VI.	Petra, the City of Shams	97
VII.	Damascus, the City of Substance	110
VIII.	Tyre, the City of Merchants	125
IX.	Athens, the City of Culture	143
X.	Rome, the City of the Law-Givers	162
XI.	Samaria, the City of Politicians	184
XII.	Susa, the City of the Satraps	205
XIII.	Jerusalem, the City of the Pharisees	227
XIV.	New Jerusalem: I. The City of God	250
XV.	New Jerusalem: II. The King	270

ANCIENT CITIES.

I.

UR, THE CITY OF SAINTS.

A GLANCE at the map of Asia shows the great plain of Mesopotamia shaped like a slender wedge, ending in a blunted point a little north of the Persian Gulf. The south portion of this wedge was ancient Chaldæa or Babylonia. The extent of the region included in that name is not accurately known. It appears to have reached somewhat north of Bagdad, and to have contained an area about equal to that of New England, minus Maine and Vermont.

The northern half of the district was originally called Accad, the southern Sumir or Shinar, and its primitive inhabitants are known to scholars as Accadians, or more correctly Sumir-Accadians.

To-day this region strikes the eye as probably the most desolate that has ever been inhabited by men. The Arabian desert presses it upon the west, while a sterile waste divides it from the mountains of Elam upon the east. Southward the space between the rivers consists of marshes, which are at times a morass, at times a parched bottom festering in ulcers of putrescent mire. Huge mounds covered wholly or in part by drifts from the desert emphasize the desolation. These occur at irregular intervals on both sides of the Euphrates, and some of them might easily be mistaken for enormous sand heaps. They are really the rejected shells in which the civilization of Christendom germinated. In them human history appears to have begun. At least it has not yet been traced beyond them, and Dr. Hommel has made it appear probable that even the Nile received the seeds of her civilization from the Euphrates.

Each of these desolate mounds was once a city. Four thousand years before Christ, some of them contained temples, observatories, libraries, with written laws and a literature of which some is still preserved.

When fragments of burnt clay, bricks, and tiles covered with curious markings were first observed among these sand heaps, the markings were mistaken for ornamental work. Soon seen to be too regular for that, it was conjectured that they might be inscriptions, but if so they were in a language of which no man living knew a letter. The history of the processes by which the inscriptions were deciphered and their language mastered records one of the most amazing triumphs of the human mind. The language can now be read almost as accurately as Hebrew or Greek.

Some of the clay fragments proved to be parts of books, some public documents, some business contracts, some magical charms, some hymns and prayers, and some astronomical records. The origin of the people who have left these enduring memorials is not yet determined. It is highly probable that like all the most virile nations they were an amalgamation of many races.

Six miles west of the Euphrates and more than a hundred north of the Persian Gulf lies the mound which was once Ur of the Chaldees. In Abraham's day it was a harbor on the Gulf, and the Euphrates swept its walls, for the ocean has been steadily retreating and the Euphrates moving eastward at rates approximately known. The surrounding country, now so desolate, was then a garden. Irrigated by human skill, the land was surpassingly fertile. Ships filled the harbor, and the ancestors of Jacob bargained in the streets.

To us the most interesting object in the city was a temple dedicated to the God of the Moon. Two stories of this temple were discovered by Mr. Loftus still standing above the mound, the only Chaldæan temple yet found which had not been buried beneath rubbish.

Like all the early Chaldæan temples, this one at Ur was built in rectangular stages rising like a terrace in diminishing size, the corners directed with mathematical accuracy toward the cardinal points. The walls of the ground stage were enormously thick, and buttressed to sustain the superincumbent weight. They inclosed a solid filling, and formed the first of an unknown number of stories which appear to have served chiefly as a pedestal for the shrine which surmounted the structure, and which was reached by an external stairway or possibly by an inclined plane running around the outer surface of the building. The walls of the shrine were probably adorned with plates of gold and silver and polished agate. The image of the Moon

God, a seated figure beneath a crescent, may have appeared upon it, but more probably only a short column of black stone inscribed with a star. Here, however, was the observatory, where nightly the heavens were watched and the observations recorded in soft clay afterwards baked in fire or hardened in the sun. For every Chaldæan temple was also an observatory. The ground stage was built of bricks cemented with bitumen, and the bricks were inscribed with the name of the monarch by whom it was erected.

Not later than twenty-two centuries before Christ — how much earlier we cannot safely say — a religious revival occurred in southern Chaldæa. Its exponent was one of the most famous monarchs revealed by the cuneiform inscriptions. Until very recently he was the earliest known to them. A signet of his time is now in the British Museum. It is a small cylinder of green jasper finely cut in intaglio with four figures, of which one appears to represent the Moon God, and bears an inscription which, though not yet fully deciphered, contains the king's name and seems to mark the seal as belonging to one of his viceroys. The delicacy and sharpness of the cutting implies the use of emery. The monarch's signature is well known. It exists upon innumerable bricks from the temples he built, and has been variously read Urukh, Ourkam, Lig-Bagas, Ur-Bagas, and Urea.

Before his day the cities of southern Chaldæa had been, like those of Greece, independent of each other. Lig-Bagas united them under one rule. He ranked as the oldest of Chaldæan kings until the date of Sargon, King of Agade, — seals of whose period have also been found, and are quite similar to that already described, except that the figures carved upon them are different, — was fixed by Assyriologists at 3800 B. C. Within six years M. de Sarzec has discovered at Tell-loh, forty-five miles from Ur, statues and inscriptions which appear to have been carved at a still earlier time.

Although Lig-Bagas appears to have been a successful soldier, what distinguishes his work is its religious character. His zeal in building temples equaled that of Mahomet in destroying them. He is known as "The Builder," and although his inscription occurs more frequently than that of any other king before Nebuchadnezzar, he appears to have built temples chiefly; neither sepulchres like the kings of Egypt, nor palaces like the kings of Assyria, nor fortifications like the kings of Babylon. The bricks bearing his signature belonged to temples, and have been found in few other structures. Each temple was, as has been said, an observatory, for the warfare between ignorance and knowledge had not yet been defined as "The conflict of Religion and Science."

This monarch made Ur his capital. The Moon God was the patron deity of the city. The name of the deity was Sin, and his worship, spreading at an early date from Ur through Arabia, appears to have given its name to the most sacred mountain known to history, Sinai or the Mount of Sin.

It will interest Bible students to remember that when Abraham with his father came forth from Ur of the Chaldees to go into the land of Canaan they halted in Haran, and there remained until Terah died. Why this delay? No one could offer a reasonable conjecture until a clay cylinder written by a king of Babylon five centuries before Christ, and found a few years ago, informed us that from immemorial time Haran had been the other chief centre of the Moon God's worship in Mesopotamia, second only to Ur. There stood in Terah's day the black stone inscribed with the star which it is probable Terah had worshiped from his childhood. It seems as if the old man, driven from his home by the growth of convictions given to make his son the apostle of a truer faith, faltered at sight of the familiar emblems he had forsaken. He was not strong enough to master the reviving memories they suggested, but lingered at Haran in the clasp of old associations until death set him free.

Every religion which is not rooted in the family affections is to be distrusted, and it harmonizes with the well-known character of Abraham, and with the faith of which he was the founder, that he should have waited with his old father in Haran "until Terah died."

At the period when Ur emerges into history her religion was a system of magic, passing into polytheism. But there are early traces of a school which worshiped one supreme God. There are indications also of a fierce conflict of religions, in southern Babylonia. It may well be that Abraham was driven into exile on account of his monotheistic convictions. This would accord with the traditions of Mesopotamia, some of which are adopted in the Koran, that the patriarch was forced to fly from his father's house because he would not engage in his father's business, which was the manufacture of idols, and that he was cast into a furnace because he would not worship them.

It has been suggested that as the Assyrians and the Hebrews belonged to the same family, while the Sumirians or people of Ur belonged to a different race, the colony which settled on the Tigris may have left upper Chaldæa at the same period when Abraham went forth to Canaan. However that may be, the history of the conquest of southern Europe by barbarians was anticipated in Mesopotamia. When the Shemites took possession of Babylonia they were a rude, uncivilized race. Mastered by the mental superiority of the cultivated people they had subdued, they adopted their civilization, and in due time won renown under the imperial names of Nineveh and Babylon.

Assyria with her Semiramis, Babylon with her Nebuchadnezzar, are the names which most powerfully affect the imagination when we think of ancient empires. Each had a great career and has left a gorgeous memory. Both derived their greatness from the people represented by Ur, as Christendom received the germs of its faith from one of the citizens of Ur.

The speech of that people had become a dead language more than a thousand years before the birth of Nebuchadnezzar. A new tongue supplanted it in Chaldæa. But it remained until the age of Alexander throughout Mesopotamia the language of all learning, as Latin was the language of learning in mediæval Europe.

It was as necessary for Sennacherib to understand Accadian as for Henry VIII. to know Latin. The Bible and prayer-book used by Tiglath-pileser and Evil-merodach in Nineveh and Babylon were written by pious men in the language of Ur, a millennium before the foundations of Nineveh were laid. They had been rendered into Assyrian as our Scriptures have been translated from the Hebrew. To the time of Cyrus the Sumiro-Accadian remained the language of law, of science, of religion. Tables used in mathematics and astronomy had been compiled in it, eclipses had been calculated and the spots on the sun noted by those who spoke it before Abraham's time. The divisions of the day into twenty-four hours, of the year into months, the signs of the zodiac, the names of the planets, the system of weights and measures employed throughout the world until the age of Alexander, the alphabets of Phœnicia and of Greece, and probably of Egypt, came from the same source. The skillful system of irrigation by canals and water wheels which gave to Mesopotamia a fertility almost unequaled was invented by the same ingenious people, and from them Babylon learned to cut gems with a skill which five centuries before Christ could be equaled nowhere else.

For more than two thousand years the region of which Ur was once the capital was regarded as a holy land. No tombs of an age so old as Nineveh have been found in northern Mesopotamia. It is a question where the Assyrians buried their dead. It has been inferred from the discovery of jars containing calcined bones, that the Babylonians practiced incremation. The conjecture has even been hazarded that the furnace of Daniel which was heated seven times hotter than it was wont to be heated may have been one of those used for that purpose. But it would be difficult to conceive of three men walking with " the form of the fourth" in such a structure, and that cremation was practiced at all by the ancient Assyrians is not yet proved.

The hypothesis of Mr. Loftus is more plausible. Kerbella is a modern Moslem town near the Euphrates. There the Moslem martyr Husseyn was buried. For that reason it still is counted holy ground. Interment there is believed to expiate all sins. The vilest criminal is supposed to be sure of heaven if his bones are buried at Kerbella. Corpses by tens of thousands are carried thither for interment every year.

For two millenniums the same sentiment appears to have prevailed regarding the land of Ur. No cemeteries of unquestionable antiquity have been discovered elsewhere in Mesopotamia. In southern Babylonia are vast cities of the dead: miles upon miles of corpses inclosed in clay coffins, the skeleton fingers clutching copper drinking cups, and metal plates upon which traces of food are still apparent. Interspersed with sepulchres of masonry, the coffins lie side by side in strata one above another, beginning below the natural surface of the ground rising at times sixty feet above it, threaded with drains skillfully arranged to carry off moisture, and flues to allow the escape of gases, in numbers beyond all computation. These cities of the dead, more populous than the cemeteries of the Nile, extending unmeasured distances into the desert, their boundaries as yet unknown, were probably the campo santo to which for two millenniums the dead were brought upon the water ways of the Tigris and Euphrates.

Another fact may illustrate the sanctity attributed to Ur, while it draws us towards an ancient people with a fellowship of human sympathy.

Amid the ruins of the temple of the Moon God were found four duplicate clay cylinders placed there by Nabonidus, the last king of Babylon. Each informs us that the monarch whose name it bears repaired the temple as an act of piety, and concludes with a prayer that his piety may be rewarded by blessings upon Belshazzar the son of his heart. This was the Belshazzar whose miserable end is described in the Book of Daniel. Before the discovery of this cylinder there appeared to be an irreconcilable conflict between the scriptural statement that Belshazzar was the last king of Babylon, and Berosus, by whom Nabonidus was said to be the last king of that city. The two statements are reconciled, and the remarkable fact that in Dan. v. 7 the position next the throne is referred to as that of the third ruler in the kingdom explained, by the discovery that Belshazzar was the son of Nabonidus, and that the two were probably associated as colleagues.

A distinctive institution of the people of Ur was the Sabbath. From them it was derived by the Assyrians. The people of Ur called it "the day of completed labors," and the phrase reminds us of a fact usually forgotten by those most zealous in trying to enforce the commandment from the Decalogue, namely, that the first and perhaps most important half of it reads, "Six days shalt thou labor."

The Assyrians called it the "day of rest for the heart," and this is one of the few traces of gentleness found in the records of that fierce nation. Minute directions for the observance of the day, translated from the old Accadian, the language of Ur, are written on the clay prayer-books of Nineveh. On the seventh day "flesh cooked by fire may not be eaten, the clothing of the body may not be changed; white garments may not be put on, a sacrifice may not be offered, the king may not ride in his chariot, nor speak in public. The augur may not mutter in a secret place, medicine to the body may not be applied, nor any curse uttered."

The command given by Moses begins, "*Remember*" the Sabbath day, as if the lawgiver was not instituting a new observance, but reënforcing an old one, which had been forgotten or neglected. The reason is plain when we reflect that Abraham came from Ur.

At Ur slaves enjoyed the protection of law. Woman was regarded as the equal of man. In domestic affairs she took precedence. The Assyrians were not pleased by this. Their libraries have furnished a vast number of clay tablets on which the old Accadian literature is translated in parallel columns into the Assyrian vernacular. It is amusing to observe that whenever the words "men" and "women" occur coupled together, the ancient language reads "women and men," while the Assyrian translation invariably inverts the order and writes "men and women." The position Sarah occupied in Abraham's household, and the deference with which he yielded to her wishes, even when it wrung his heart to do so, may indicate the training of his youth.

A dark feature in the religion of Accad may not be passed in silence. It permitted human sacrifice. In certain rare and extreme emergencies the son might be offered as a victim to God by the father. "The son's eyes for the father's eyes, the son's heart for the father's heart, the son's life for the father's life, the father must give."

The Bible tells us how the faithful Abraham was delivered from that darkest of superstitions.

When the voice of God had restrained the patriarch from the intended slaughter of Isaac, the promise of future blessings came to him in words whose whole significance depended upon the recollections of a childhood during which he may have watched from the temple at Ur the stars trooping in endless procession overhead and the waves breaking upon the broad beach beneath him: "In blessing I will bless thee, and in multiplying I will multiply thee *as the stars of the heaven*, and as *the sand which is upon the sea-shore*."

This brief review of Ur reminds us that the strongest influences upon earth are those exerted by men acting under religious inspirations. From the land of Ur came forth the power which made Assyria great, the wisdom which until a period comparatively recent made the word "Chaldæan" a synonym for intellectual superiority, and from the same city of saints led by a religious inspiration came also the patriarch whose faith, purified by trial and strengthened by conflict, shone at last in the face of Jesus which is the Christ.

II.

NINEVEH, THE CITY OF SOLDIERS.

Nineveh was the most warlike city known to history. We cannot except even Sparta, which might have served as a closet in one of her royal residences. The site of Nineveh is marked by the modern town of Mosul. It seems the irony of history that the place renowned throughout the ancient world for its skill in clothing men in iron should be famous throughout the modern world for its skill in clothing women in gauze.

Nineveh stands in our thoughts for Assyria, because she was the capital of that empire during the whole period of its grandeur. In childhood we were fascinated by the classic stories of Assyrian history. They began with the mysterious Queen Semiramis building the tomb in memory of her husband Ninus. They ended with Sardanapalus, the Sybarite king, who wore women's clothes and wasted his days in splendid sloth until his palace was besieged; fought like a lion at last, and, before his defenses fell, gathered his wives, his concubines, his children, and his treasures in one funeral pyre; covered it with spices; commanded the lutes to play and the singers to sing while his own hand applied the torch, and so perished amid commingling sounds of lute and trumpet and song and battle-shriek, choked with smoke and smothered in perfumes. These fables had been widely diffused by Rossini's opera and Byron's tragedy, when the school of Max Müller assured us that the suicide and the flaming pyre were, like the story of the dying Hercules, only one of the many forms assumed by the myth of the setting sun; and now the voice of that school is silenced by the cuneiform inscriptions. While the Assyrian monuments have disproved much of the classic story, they have confirmed parts of it, and have revealed facts more marvelous by far than the fables they have superseded.

Campaigns briefly alluded to in the Bible are minutely described in the excavated records. Where the long buried inscriptions and the Scripture narratives touch, they fit into each other as tenons into mortises cut to receive them. Thus, the monuments inform us that Sennacherib did not invade Judæa a second time, but do not give the reason. The Bible tells us that his first invasion ended in irreparable disaster. The Bible says that Sennacherib was murdered by his sons, but leaves us to conjecture the motives of his murderers. The monuments describe the murder and the causes which led to it. A clay tablet preserved in the British Museum contains the monarch's will. He bequeathed his treasures to his youngest son, Esar-haddon. That jealousy impelled the elder brothers to rebellion and patricide is no longer conjecture, but history.

The Bible affirms that the king of Assyria carried Manasseh in chains to *Babylon*. But Babylon was not the capital of Assyria, and the statement sounded as if we should read that Napoleon carried his prisoners to London. Before the critics had ceased emphasizing this supposed inaccuracy of Scripture, the monuments revealed that one, and one only, in the long line of Assyrian kings had made Babylon a royal residence, and held court there during a part of every year. This king, the same Esar-haddon, was the monarch who is said in the Bible to have transported Manasseh from Jerusalem.

It once appeared that the tenth chapter of Isaiah could not have been written by the author of the thirty-sixth and thirty-eventh chapters, because the statements of the two passages contradicted each other. Both describe an invasion by Assyria. But the tenth describes minutely the approach of the invaders to Jerusalem by a route which the later chapters show that the Assyrians carefully avoided. It also implies that Jerusalem was taken, while the later chapters declare explicitly that Jerusalem was not taken. These apparent contradictions were explained by the decipherment of an inscription recording an invasion of which scholars had not dreamed. It occurred ten years before that of Sennacherib, and was conducted by his father Sargon, an abler general and a greater man. The same inscription informs us that Sargon passed through the places named in the tenth of Isaiah, and that he captured Jerusalem.

The excavated monuments are the most valuable commentaries upon those parts of the Bible which touch Mesopotamian history. They have fixed many important Biblical dates with accuracy and certainty, and the most bewildering chapter of Holy

Writ, the first of Ezekiel, becomes luminous to the reader who will but glance over the plates in which the palaces of Nineveh have been depicted by Rich, Botta, or Layard.

Assur was the early capital of Assyria. An inscription has been found written by one of the sovereigns who reigned there about 1330 B. C. But Tiglath-Pileser I. is the earliest distinctly outlined national hero. Memorials of his conquests have been found as far west as the island of Cyprus. He lived in the twelfth century B. C., and made Nineveh an important city in a powerful empire.

Beginning as a band of loosely organized robbers, the Assyrians were slowly compacted into a strong nation and attained their greatest grandeur in the second empire, which was founded by a usurper named Pul.

This man appears to have begun life as a gardener. He seized the sceptre after the manner of the great Corsican, assumed the name of the national hero, and ascended the throne as Tiglath-Pileser II., April 30, B. C. 745. The most splendid period of Nineveh was a little less than a century later.

East of the Tigris, and north of its junction with the river Zab, are four huge mounds. They mark approximately the corners of a parallelogram, of which the north and south diagonal is about twenty, and the east and west about sixteen, miles in length. The most westerly of these mounds lies upon the bank of the Tigris opposite Mosul, and is without doubt the site of the original Nineveh.

Opinions regarding the size of the ancient city vary. The most probable and the only satisfactory supposition seems to be that the whole territory included between the four mounds, with a still larger space beyond them, was at one time described by its name. The kings of Assyria were possessed by a mania for building palaces. Each of her greatest monarchs built one for himself, located it a few miles from the palace of his predecessor, fortified and made it his capital. A new city grew up around each royal residence, and when the suburbs of these several cities touched each other, they formed a vast metropolis, covering a space larger than London and only a little smaller than the later Babylon. This is the only theory which explains the Biblical and classical traditions of the vast size of Nineveh, provides space for the immense park the city is known to have contained, and at the same time accounts for the fact that the bricks in each of the several mounds are inscribed with the legends of different builders. The whole of this vast territory which I venture to include in the name of Nineveh was probably fortified, while each section would necessarily appear, as it actually does, a separate fortress defended with equal care on every side. The palace of Sennacherib stood in the oldest quarter, which may be conceived as bearing some such relation to the whole metropolis as " the City " sustains to London.

Of this original Nineveh the Tigris formed the western boundary. For two and a half miles along the bank, west of the palace which was itself almost a fortress, ran a stupendous wall, flanked by frequent towers and pierced for gateways. Each gateway opened between colossal stone sculptures of lions or bulls with human faces and eagle wings. The sculptures faced outwards, and were considered the guardian deities of the place. A succession of several parallel walls, with moats between them, protected the eastern approach, and similar defenses guarded the city on the north, while the Khausar stream was skillfully used to protect it on the south. Thus, like each section of the ultimate Nineveh, it could be taken only by a separate siege.

The streets were paved with blocks of limestone, which show to-day the deep ruts worn by war chariots twenty-five centuries ago. They rang with the tramp of soldiers marching in iron armor, with scarlet shields and mantles. The men were of larger limb and stature, and more muscular, than any other known members of the Semite race. Their patron deity was Nin, the original of the Greek Hercules. They worshiped strength, and would say their prayers only to colossal idols of stone, lions and bulls whose ponderous limbs, eagle wings, and human heads were symbols of strength, courage, and victory. Fighting was the business of the nation, and the priests were incessant fomenters of war. They were supported largely from the spoils of conquest, of which a fixed percentage was invariably assigned them before others shared, for this race of plunderers was excessively religious.

The shops of the city were furnished with all the appliances of luxury which the world could supply. No ladies appeared in the streets, for women were rigorously secluded.

The gentlemen wore embroidered mantles, and carried canes topped with delicate carvings in ivory, agate, or emerald.

The palace of Sennacherib stood upon an enormous artificial mound, which covered a hundred acres. It has been estimated that the labor of 20,000 men for six years was required to raise the mound alone, and an inscription of Sennacherib boasts that he employed captives from Chaldæa in rebuilding the palace upon it.

The palace itself was the largest, excepting only the great structure at Karnak, known to have been built by man. The inner surfaces of the walls, gleaming with facings of enameled bricks, blue, orange, and red, were more gorgeous than those of Venice in her prime. The magnificent gateways, approached by flights of marble steps, were flanked with towers and guarded by the perpetually recurring winged bulls and lions. The glory of the palace was in the majestic halls it contained. These were of unknown height, and varied in length between one and two hundred feet. They were alike except in size. Their floors were of marble inlaid with metal arabesques. The upper parts of the walls were faced with brilliantly enameled bricks, and the lower paneled high as the eye could read with alabaster slabs covered with sculptures. The sculptures illustrate Assyrian history. Sieges are depicted, battles portrayed, with the names of the monarchs who won them. These halls appear to have been open to the public, and in them Assyrian boys probably received their most effectual education.

An inscription informs us that in the year 883 B. C. Assur-nizir-pal conquered the city of Tela, cut off the hands, feet, ears, and noses of its inhabitants, put out their eyes, raised two mounds outside the city, one of human heads and one of human limbs, and burned all the children in fire.

A sculpture presents the king on his throne, grasping a spear, with which he is putting out the eyes of prisoners led before him by thongs fastened to hooks inserted in their jaws.

We read in the Bible that Sennacherib took Lachish. A set of sculptures in his palace shows us the monarch on a throne before that city reviewing the captives as they are driven before him. The history of the campaign is written on his cylinder. It tells of men impaled, flayed alive, tortured in nameless ways. The sound of Nahum's curse, " Woe to the bloody city," reached our ears long before we discovered the boastful words in which the scribes of Sennacherib recorded the horrible facts by which it was elicited. The palace of Assur-bani-pal was built upon the same mound on which that of his grandfather Sennacherib stood. It contained the public library. The checks in baked clay, used by the people of Nineveh in drawing books, have been found among the ruins. Tablets found here contain an inscription such as Bacon or Franklin might have written, to the effect that knowledge is power, for the seeing eye, the hearing ear, are the foundation of greatness. Here could be seen in baked clay, or at times perhaps in papyrus, the bulletins often sent by generals in the field, and the fortnightly reports from the observatories throughout the empire. The latter were sufficiently minute to note the spots upon the sun.

The literature of Nineveh consisted mainly of translations from the classic Sumir-Accadian. In the library of Assur-bani-pal was found that ancient epic, composed more than two millenniums before Christ, which relates the adventures of the mythical Gisdubar, adventures which, vivified in later ages by the genius of Greece, have come down to us in classic forms as the twelve labors of Hercules.

The same library has given us a copy of the old Accadian laws, the oldest code known in the world. It affords protection to slaves, and requires officiating magistrates to renew each day their oaths to administer the laws with justice. Here Sir Henry Rawlinson discovered the Assyrian canon, which makes it possible to certify dates in the history of that people with accuracy. The Assyrians preserved their chronology by naming each year after some well-known official. The first year of the cycle bore, it might be, the name of the reigning sovereign. The next that of his chief general, and so on in an established order. Thus, pride kept the calendar correct. To give his name to the year might be a man's only chance of immortality. The discovery of this catalogue of name-years, reaching back to the beginning of the tenth century B. C., was perhaps the most valuable discovery yet made in Mesopotamia.

The library of Assur-bani-pal was also a court of records. Very many contracts inscribed in clay have been brought from it to the British Museum and there deciphered.

One informs us that July 20, 709 B. C., a Phœnician trader sold to a lady of Nineveh two Hebrew slaves. Price $135, $1,350 forfeit if not delivered within a specified time. The price of real estate is known from deeds in clay deposited in the same place. A house was sold on the 16th of May, 692 B. C., in Nineveh for $45.

After centuries of almost perpetual war, the rate of interest 700 B. C. was at Nineveh only four per cent., and for copper three per cent. The fact reminds us that the nations of the old world could afford to be always fighting, if only they were victorious. The spoils of victory paid the bills.

Among the most interesting tablets from Nineveh are primers prepared for children. One of these tells us it was specially designed to teach the king's granddaughter to spell. Many of these inscriptions, written in letters so fine that a magnifying glass is required to read them, suggest that one was used in writing them. Since one lens, much warped by the action of fire, has already been found, it is not improbable that others may be discovered.

The great park of Nineveh was probably laid out by Tiglath-Pileser I. He designed it for a botanical garden. By him it was planted with exotics brought from the various lands he had conquered. In a later age it served as the royal hunting-ground. The chase was the recreation, as war was the business, of the Assyrian monarchs, and when luxury had made them too indolent or too effeminate to hunt among the mountains, they indulged their taste by slaughtering wild beasts, which had been caught and kept in cages for the purpose.

Not many years before the fall of Nineveh a military pageant moved through its streets. The army had returned from a successful campaign in the east. The king visited the temple to give thanks in the presence of all his army. We can conceive the sight. The soldiers marched with scarlet shields and glittering spears. The splendid war chariots, the terror of the old world, the artillery of ancient warfare, appeared in line. They were of iron, richly embossed, and gorgeous with dashes of vermillion. Each bore a nobleman armed with bow and quiver, and protected by a huge shield held before him. The charioteer stood behind and guided the steeds by long leathern reins. But the most conspicuous chariot in the pageant is not drawn by horses. It contains a single occupant. He is his own charioteer. It is Assur-bani-pal, the Sardanapalus of Greek history. He wears a lofty crown not unlike that of the Vatican. His close-fitting mantle is richly embroidered, probably with gold and gems, though that the sculptures do not clearly show. The reins are studded with gold bosses; and the steeds harnessed in silver chains before the chariot are four captive kings.

An elaborate sculpture shows the same monarch in the palace garden banqueting with his queen. The king reclines upon a couch, his limbs covered with a robe of rich embroidery. The queen is seated in a high-backed chair. They are pledging each other in goblets of ornamented gold. Musicians appear among the trees playing on several different kinds of instruments, and, pendent from the branches above, hangs the head of a king. "Woe to the bloody city."

The announcement by Sennacherib upon his cylinder, that he had salted and packed in baskets the heads of his captives, which he had doubtless sent to decorate the walls of the capital, seems to have excited no surprise. "Woe to the bloody city."

At last when every nation from Egypt and Lydia to Persia had been outraged by the warriors of Nineveh; when successive conquerors, Tiglath-Pileser, Sargon, Sennacherib, had died in the field or perished by assassination, the inevitable end came. A coalition similar to that which overwhelmed the first Napoleon was formed against Assyria. Nabopolassar, the ablest Assyrian general then living, played the rôle of Murat by deserting to the enemy. Saracus, the last Assyrian king, was besieged in his capital. For more than two years the invincible city resisted. Then occurred an unprecedented flood in the Tigris. The enemy still pressed the siege. The river wall of the palace was undermined and fell. Nineveh was taken. The king fired his own palace and perished in the flames.

With the overthrow of Nineveh the Assyrian nation vanished. At the date of her greatest power, when her kings were feared throughout Asia more than Napoleon was ever feared by Europe, one statesman in an obscure province of the empire saw the seeds of her ruin ripening, and cried in the ears of his frightened countrymen: "Fear her not, for God is against her. Nineveh! thy crowned ones are as the locusts, and thy captains as the great grasshoppers which camp in the hedges in the cold day, but when the sun is arisen they fly away and their place is not known where they are."

Within sixty years the prediction was fulfilled. Three centuries later Alexander fought the battle of Arbela within sight of the mounds of Nineveh and saw no suggestions of a city there. Nine centuries later the battle which prepared Western Asia to become Mahometan was fought upon the site of Nineveh, and neither of the contending armies knew they were treading above the streets of a buried metropolis. A millennium later, Niebuhr, in charge of an expedition sent to explore the ruins of Nineveh, passed over its site without a suspicion that he had reached it. But the stones at last have spoken, and have given in their testimony to the truthfulness of Him who said: "They that take the sword shall perish by the sword." "The meek shall inherit the earth."

III.

BABYLON, THE CITY OF SENSUALISTS.

Two observations seem to be required by way of preface to the following paper : —

1. The description given of the size of Babylon and the magnitude of its walls rests upon the testimony of eyewitnesses, and is credited by the weightiest authorities at the present day. It has been doubted by modern writers of repute, not because the proof is weak, but because the facts are marvelous. They appear so to those familiar only with modern times. But they are scarcely surprising to those whose minds have dwelt among ages and peoples where a single will controlled amounts of naked human labor which were practically unlimited. Mr. Grote indorses the statement that the Chinese wall alone contains more material than all the buildings in the British Empire. If we could enter the Babylon of Nebuchadnezzar after driving our carriage twelve hundred miles along the top of that wall, or even after scaling one of the pyramids, we should not be greatly astonished at sight of the city described by Herodotus.

2. I make no attempt to fix the date or the authorship of Daniel. I think Ewald was correct in assigning it to the age of the Maccabees. Dean Milman, who holds the same opinion, believes in the accuracy of its historic statements. Cuneiform discovery has

confirmed those statements at several points, and justifies, as I think the following paper will show, the impression that the author of the Book, whoever he may have been, and in whatever age he may have lived, possessed information of which the classical authorities were ignorant. The source of that information cannot here be discussed.

Babylon was old before Nineveh was born. It was one of the earliest and most important cities of that Accadian race which founded " Ur of the Chaldees." Cuneiform inscriptions have identified it as the Babel of Genesis, and record a tradition of the tower builded there which varies little from that contained in the Bible. The name " Babil," which signified in the primitive tongue " Gate of God," resembled in sound the Hebrew word meaning " Confusion," and was, therefore, incorporated in the Scriptural narrative as having that significance.

During the whole period of Ninevite supremacy, Babylon ranked as an important city. As the source of science, literature, and especially religion, she held precedence of Nineveh. She was aureoled with something of that religious reverence which gilded Rome during the Middle Ages, and while subject to Nineveh nursed that fierce scorn of her conquerors which intellect naturally feels for brute force; the contempt of the Greek for the barbarian, of the Jew for the Gentile. Though conquered and occupied at a very early period by the same race which ruled from Nineveh, and though Assyria was probably a colony which left Babylonia about the time when Abraham left Ur, Babylon was more closely bound than Nineveh in the great traditions of the Accadians.

The earliest king in Babylonia whose date is known was Sargon of Agade. His date has been fixed at 3800 B. C. on the evidence of an inscription by Nabonidus, the last independent king of Babylon, in which Nabonidus placed the reign of Sargon 3,200 years before his own. A small oval of hard pinkish gray stone inscribed by this Sargon was found by Mr. Rassam. It is now in the British Museum. The stone is drilled, polished, and cut with a skill which implies a high degree of culture, and the letters are of the kind employed after the primitive picture writing had ceased to be used, and before the later cuneiform letters had been developed into their ultimate forms. The legendary history of Sargon bears a remarkable similarity to that of Moses. He is said to have been placed by his mother immediately after his birth in an ark of rushes, and abandoned to the waters of the Euphrates, whence he was rescued and became a great monarch.

Babylon was conquered by Tiglath-Pileser I. about 1100 B. C., and remained in partial or complete subjection to Assyria during much of the period between the reign of that monarch and the fall of Nineveh. By Sennacherib it was almost entirely destroyed and left little more than a heap of ruins.

While the coalition which overwhelmed Nineveh was forming, Nabopolassar, the ablest Assyrian general then living, was sent by the king of Nineveh to Babylon to quell an insurrection there. He betrayed his sovereign by putting himself at the head of the rebels he had been sent to subdue, joined the allies in their attack upon Nineveh, usurped the throne he had helped to empty, transferred the capital from Nineveh to Babylon, and so founded about 610 B. C. the great Babylonian Empire, which soon came to be Assyria enlarged, under a new name and an abler ruler.

Nabopolassar was succeeded by his son Nebuchadnezzar. That monarch, a brilliant general, an able statesman, a magnificent patron of the arts and sciences, was a profoundly religious man. He united in himself the functions of general, king, and pope. His ambition equaled his ability. Inheriting a kingdom scarcely larger than Portugal, he extended its limits over most of the then known world. The historic Babylon was purely his creation. His power was autocratic, and he could have said more truthfully than Louis XIV., "I am the State." By an almost universal conquest, he inaugurated a general peace, and although the Hebrew prophet called him " the Hammer of the whole earth," he strove to retain in cords of silk the nations which Nineveh had bound in fetters of iron. His supreme ambition was to make Babylon what Napoleon strove to render Paris, — the incomparable metropolis of the world. Hence it came to pass that history records, perhaps, no other reign so lavishly adorned as his with both the triumphs of war and the splendors of peace. Vast resources enabled him to accomplish his designs. He had drained the treasuries of all the richest nations into his own, and taken captive an almost unlimited number of men to labor in executing his great works.

The timber of Lebanon was his. The clay and bitumen beneath his feet supplied unlimited materials for building. The fleets of Phœnicia sailed at his orders. They brought him gold, iron, and tin, from Africa, Spain, and England. Their mariners, transported to the Euphrates, navigated his ships to India and Ceylon, and returned with gems, pearls, spices, and precious woods. The camels of Arabia bore his freights across the desert. The science and skill of Chaldæa were at his command to make the most effective use of his resources. These were some of the facilities which enabled him to make "this great Babylon," which he "built by the might of his power and for the glory of his majesty," "the Lady of Kingdoms, the Glory of the Chaldees' Excellency, the Joy of the whole Earth."

Though Nebuchadnezzar could be cruel when he considered cruelty expedient, his impulses were kind. He adopted a policy more enlightened than that which Assyria had pursued, and endeavored to perpetuate his empire by cultivating commerce and the arts of peace. By his marriage with a Median princess he gained the friendship of the only people he could not conquer, the brave

BABYLON, THE CITY OF SENSUALISTS. 41

mountaineers, who may be justly called the Swiss of ancient Asia.

The Babylon of Nebuchadnezzar occupied a square of which each side was nearly fifteen miles in length, and was bisected by the Euphrates diagonally from northwest to southeast. This square was inclosed by a deep moat, flooded from the river. The clay excavated in digging the moat, moulded into bricks and laid in bitumen, formed the walls of the city. These walls, more than three hundred feet high and more than seventy thick, and protected by parapets, afforded a commodious driveway along their top of nearly sixty miles, needing only aerial bridges over the Euphrates river. The waters of the river were forced to flow through the city between quays of masonry which equaled the walls in thickness and height. The walls were pierced at equal intervals for a hundred gates, and each gateway closed with double leaves of ponderous metal, swinging upon bronze posts built into the wall. Fifty broad avenues, crossing each other at right angles, joined the opposite gates of the city, and divided it into a checkerboard of gigantic squares. The river quays were pierced by twenty-five gates like those in the outer walls. One of the streets was carried across the river upon an arched bridge, another ran in a tunnel beneath the river bed, and ferries plied continually across the water where the other streets abutted.

The great squares of the city were not all occupied by buildings. Many of them were used as gardens and even farms, and the great fertility of the soil, caused by irrigation, producing two and even three crops a year, supplied food sufficient for the inhabitants in case of siege. Babylon was a vast fortified province rather than a city.

On the right of the Euphrates, in Borsippa, I think within the walls, stood the Temple of the Spheres. Its foundations had been laid by an earlier king, but the building was erected by Nebuchadnezzar. It arose, like the Temple of the Moon God at Ur, in a succession of seven rectangular stages or platforms, of which the lowest was 272 feet, and the highest twenty feet, square. The sides of each platform were faced with bricks, gorgeously colored and glazed. The ground stage, twenty-six feet high, was black like jet, the color of the planet Saturn. The next orange, Jupiter. The next blood red like ruby glass, Mars. The next was covered with plates of burnished gold, in honor of the sun. Above this, pale yellow, Venus. Mercury, deep blue, gleaming like a sapphire. The highest, plated with polished silver, represented the moon. Here stood the shrine, and here, if we may judge from the analogy of other Chaldæan temples, was the observatory, in which observations were taken with instruments of sufficient accuracy to discover the satellites of Jupiter. The building appears to have been solid, and was ascended by an inclined plane circling around its outer surface. In high lights it must have glittered like cut gems laid nearly in the order of rainbow colors, and the description of it suggests the imagery of the Apocalypse.

There is a curious fact which I do not remember to have seen noticed, and of which I will not here venture to suggest the explanation. Babylon stands in the Book of Revelation as the emblem of all the abominations which are to be destroyed by the power of Christ. But Babylon is the one city known to history which could have served as a model for John's description of the New Jerusalem: "the city lying four square," "the walls great and high," the river which flowed through the city, "and in the midst of the street of it, and on either side of the river the tree of life, bearing twelve manner of fruits;" "the foundations of the wall of the city garnished with all manner of precious stones," as the base of the walls inclosing the great palace were faced with glazed and enameled bricks of brilliant colors, and a broad space left that they might be seen, — these characteristics, and they are all unique, have been combined in no other city.

On the east of the Euphrates stood the palace of Nebuchadnezzar. Little is known of its appearance. An inscription boasts that the strong defensive walls which inclosed it were raised in fifteen days. The mention of it recalls the worst and the best traits of the great monarch's character. For here was brought that Jewish king whom Nebuchadnezzar made blind *after* slaying his two sons before his eyes. And here, too, when his Median wife longed for her native hills, Nebuchadnezzar erected the celebrated hanging gardens, to solace her homesickness with a miniature of her fatherland. Enormous arches of masonry were piled one upon another, supporting hills of earth where wild flowers nestled amid the roots of forest trees, and artificial crags down which dashed brooks, kept full from the Euphrates by water screws, used here some centuries before they were invented by Archimedes.

Among those waiting in the palace court, permit me to point out two who may any morning have been present. One is a Babylonian gentleman of leisure. Over a tunic of white linen he wears a flowing mantle, richly embroidered, and caught about the waist by a girdle studded with gems. His thick black hair and beard are carefully perfumed, and like the gentlemen of Nineveh, he carries a cane with a jeweled handle.

The other is a military officer. Instead of a mantle he wears a coat of mail. It fits him like a shirt. The sleeves reach half way to the elbows, and the skirts descend to the knees. It is formed of copper or bronze medallions, each about the size of an English penny, a little larger than an American copper cent, fastened upon leather and slightly overlapping each other like the scales of a fish. Each medallion is embossed in delicate relief with the figure of the god Bel, or Nebo, his Hermes.

The two are conversing. No telephone

can bring a conversation over twenty-three centuries, but we know the subjects which most absorbed the attention of Nebuchadnezzar's courtiers at one period of his reign, and the views they took of it. The officer has returned, we will suppose, from inspecting the great canal which joins the Euphrates with the sea, flowing five hundred miles, and is speaking of the Hebrew captives whom Nebuchadnezzar had settled along its banks. They were celebrated singers, and the Babylonians were exceptionally fond of music, as their monuments show. The officer relates that when he asked one of the slaves, whom he saw with harp in hand, for a song, the insolent fellow hung his harp upon the willows which fringed the great canal, and broke forth with a wild, sad cry: "They who have carried us away captive require of us a song! How can I sing the songs of Zion in a strange land! If I forget thee, O Jerusalem, may my right hand forget her cunning! If I remember not thee above my chief joy, may my tongue cleave to the roof of my mouth."

"But a stranger thing occurred," the officer may have continued. "When I visited the same region some time ago, I saw a young Hebrew, he seemed a mere boy, surrounded by a crowd of his countrymen. He was showing them a tile, upon which he had drawn a picture of Jerusalem besieged by our armies. It was just after Zedekiah had been crowned by our king, and no mortal imagined he would be fool enough to rebel. But this Jew, whom they called Ezechiel, declared his picture represented what was actually coming, and he should send it as a warning to the king of Jerusalem. Time proved that he was right, and strangely, too, when we took the city for the last time, we found there a very old man named Jeremiah, who for many years had been saying the same things as this Ezechiel. His countrymen had treated him sometimes as a madman, and sometimes as a traitor, but Nebuchadnezzar received him into distinguished favor."

What most excites both soldier and civilian is suggested by that last remark, the influence these Jews have gained at court. They speak of Daniel and his three friends, and express strong hopes that the approaching festival will end their influence forever.

That festival it is possible to describe

with considerable minuteness. It appears to have been the dedication of the great statue placed upon the temple of Bel. That temple, of the same general pattern as the Temple of the Spheres, was said to have been higher than the pyramid of Gizeh. The statue in the shrine upon its summit was of gold. It has been supposed that the festival described in Daniel could not have been that which occurred at the placing of this statue, because the image in Daniel is said to have been set up in the plain of Dura. But if, as Mr. Budge believes, the "plain of Dura" was one of the three districts in Babylon, each called Duru or fortress, the difficulty disappears.

The festival must have been one of great significance. Bel was the national deity. His image was to Babylon what the cross of St. George is to England, or the star spangled banner to the United States.

The monarch was the representative of Deity, and therefore the statue of the God was also the statue of the king. Pride, patriotism, and devotion combined to prompt the most extravagant display. Holiday was proclaimed. Civil and military functionaries were assembled from all parts of the empire. The different instruments mentioned in Daniel have been identified by help of sculptures from Nineveh, and prove that the leader of the orchestra understood that combination of wind and stringed instruments which is attributed to Mozart. Probably as the first rays of the rising sun flashed upon the golden image six hundred feet in air, the orchestra had orders to begin. At sound of the music the multitude were commanded to prostrate themselves in worship. The sight of the great temple, the flash of the splendid image, the sound of martial music, might well produce a sensuous excitement which would seek relief in adoration.

It is probable that the whole empire shared in these solemnities. When the golden spike which joined the Atlantic to the Pacific was driven, the instant the hammer fell was telegraphed over all the continent. No mysterious wires conveyed the signal across the plains of Chaldæa, but it is not impossible that trumpeters stationed within sight and hearing of each other spread the news five hundred miles as fast as sight and sound could carry it, for this was probably the proudest day of Nebuchadnezzar's great career. But there were three men in Babylon who would not worship him, nor " bow down before the image which Nebuchadnezzar, the king, had set up." They saw working beneath the splendor the hidden leaven of decay.

The reign of Nebuchadnezzar continued forty-three years. He left Babylon the metropolis of the world. Thither Egypt sent for sun-dials and water-clocks. Thence the ladies of the Orient received the fashions, as Christendom follows the fashions set by Paris. From Babylon Tyre took the weights and measures which regulated commerce. From Babylon the Greeks received the tables on which their science was based, and Lydia the lutes on which she learned at last to excel her teacher.

To Babylon Egypt sent her finest gold and her choicest ivory, Tyre her most gorgeous dyes, India her largest pearls, Arabia her choicest spices, Media her agates and emeralds, which nowhere else could be so finely cut. The entire vintage of Helbon was reserved for the court of Babylon, as that of Champagne was monopolized by Napoleon. Thither Greece sent her most beautiful slaves, for in Babylon a dancing-girl might be sold for the price of a year's pay to a thousand soldiers. The great Babylonian banking-house of the Egibi, whose checks and receipts in clay still exist in great numbers, occupied for five generations at Babylon the place filled in Europe by the Rothschilds since Waterloo.

But excess of luxury soon sapped the strength of Babylon's manhood. From cups of gold studded with jewels the profligate nobles drank their own death. The debaucheries into which the people sank with fearful rapidity may not be described. A law was enforced, probably the most infamous known to the annals of our race, which was designed by pandering to the grossest passion of our nature to attract strangers to Babylon by making it a paradise, or rather a stew, of sensuality. That nameless horror was conspicuous among the causes of her ruin.

Attracted by the wealth and luxury of Babylon, the Medes took possession of the city and its influence rapidly declined.

. . . .

In the present condition of cuneiform discovery it is not possible to give a description of the capture of Babylon by Cyrus. There are three sources of information.

I. Herodotus tells us that the city was besieged for some time by Cyrus, and finally taken by a stratagem, like that attempted by General Grant at Vicksburg. The river was diverted from its channel, and the besiegers entered by its dry bed at night when the gates were left carelessly open during the celebration of a religious festival. A cuneiform inscription deciphered by Sir Henry Rawlinson enabled his brother to identify with great plausibility this festival with Belshazzar's feast as described in Daniel. Professor Ewald wrote: "But among all the later reminiscences of the conquest of Babylon by Cyrus, one never-to-be-forgotten feature always rises above the rest, namely, the amazing rapidity with which the victory was gained, and the way in which the whole Chaldæan supremacy was shattered by it, at a single blow. . . . The capture of Babylon by Cyrus in a single night, while the Babylonians were celebrating in careless ease a luxurious feast, is the fixed kernel of the tradition in all its forms."

II. Inscriptions have lately been read which were written by Cyrus himself. They describe the death of Nabonidus, the last king of Babylon, and declare that Cyrus took the city without fighting; that there was no siege, but the people opened their gates and received him with joy.

III. The account in Daniel, after describing Belshazzar's feast, says only: "In that night was Belshazzar the king of the Chaldæans slain, and Darius the Mede took the kingdom." All attempts to identify this Darius have been thus far futile.

The recently deciphered cylinder of Cyrus affirms that though he entered Babylon without fighting, and was joyfully welcomed by its people, "a band of rebels" shut themselves up in a place identified as the royal palace on the left of the river, which was strongly fortified, and held out a little while against him. The little while appears to have been about four months. Professor George Rawlinson is of opinion that Belshazzar, who was then in command of the Babylonian army, with such soldiers as remained faithful, constituted "the rebels" mentioned by Cyrus, and that the feast recorded in Daniel occurred upon the night when they were captured.

We must wait for further explorations to determine whether he is correct.

What may be safely said now is this: The

tradition of the capture of Babylon, which as Professor Ewald affirms has prevailed universally from the time of Herodotus, unquestionably prevailed in the age of the Maccabees, when the Book of Daniel was probably written. The account in Daniel is not necessarily compromised by the complete overthrow of that tradition. The account of the capture of Babylon given by Cyrus himself, which was a startling surprise to scholars a few years ago, and compelled them to reconstruct all that has been written about it for more than two thousand years, except what is written in Daniel, is not inconsistent with the account given in that Book, for while the profane historians speak of Nabonidus as the last king of Babylon, and the Bible assigns that place to Belshazzar, the inscriptions give the strongest grounds for believing that the two reigned together, and allow us to believe that though the "fixed kernel" of the tradition mentioned by Ewald cannot be the capture by Cyrus of Babylon itself erroneously described by Herodotus, it may have been the capture of that vast fortified inclosure, a city within the city, correctly conceived of in Daniel.

The last memorable incident in the history of Babylon furnishes an epitome of her career from the death of Nebuchadnezzar. For there when Alexander the Great had crucified the physician who might have healed him, and had squandered fourteen million dollars in funeral orgies over the body of his friend Hephæstion, he died the death of a common drunkard, bequeathing with his latest breath, as his generals stood around him, his kingdom "To the strongest."

IV.

MEMPHIS, THE CITY OF THE DEAD.

A GREEN ribbon a thousand miles long, and varying in width from two to twelve, though rarely exceeding five; striped with a central line of umber; raveled at the northern end and the threads spread like a half-open fan; this ribbon of verdure stretched directly south from the Mediterranean upon a limitless expanse of scorching, dazzling sand, — that was Egypt, the land " in which it seemed always afternoon."

The Nile banks are a picture of life in death. Their narrow strip of fertility lies in the desert like a solitary plank in the ocean, and the earliest inhabitants, who came from Asia, appear to have felt upon it as drowning men who know they have but an hour to live.

The laws of Moses never glance at a future life. The laws of the land whence Moses came scarcely glance away from the future life. The Pentateuch leaves us doubtful whether Moses ever thought of an existence beyond the grave. The study of Egypt creates an impression that the Egyptians thought of little else. They painted their homes with pictures of heaven and hell. Their story-books relate the adventures of souls which have left their bodies. Their Robinson Crusoes and Swiss Family Robinsons are dead people. Their kindergartens taught little children charms to frighten away the dæmons that would try to hinder their souls from crossing the great desert to the throne of God, whither they must start the instant they died. Even the monarch could not be buried until a tribunal named the Court of the Dead had convened around his body and pronounced him, in the presence of forty accusers, guiltless of the sins for which it was supposed his spirit was at the same hour being tried by the unseen powers. The laws, the art, and the social manners of Egypt were calculated to impress upon the living the nearness and superlative importance of the life to come. When an Egyptian attained to his majority, he celebrated not the day of his birth, but that of his death. He began to build his tomb. There he believed his soul would often return, and there, if he were judged worthy, it would after three thousand years be reunited to his body, which must therefore be preserved for its reception.

This care for the life to come, mastering care for the life that now is, moulded the civilization of Egypt. It gave to her monuments their unique and august solemnity, and to her cast of thought a quality which makes the attempts at humor in her literature affect us as if we had seen the monkeys she trained to gather her vintages, plucking grapes in the shadow of the pyramids.

This consciousness of life in death is presented most impressively at Memphis, the earliest capital and the permanent religious centre of the land of the Pharaohs. All the grandeur of the Nile was born at Memphis and buried at Alexandria.

Memphis was the abode of the sacred bull, in which deity was believed to be incarnate. Its birthday was the Egyptian Christmas. Its image in gold, bronze, or ivory was the Egyptian's crucifix. The "golden calf" cast by Aaron in the wilderness was one of its effigies.

At Memphis it is probable that Abraham was welcomed by Pharaoh, and Joseph received his father Jacob.

The city stood on the west bank of the Nile, a few miles above the present apex of the delta, near Cairo, which has been built of materials taken from its ruins. Except the cemetery, scarcely a trace of the old metropolis remains. The Necropolis lay on the west of the city, separated from it by an artificial lake. Every Egyptian corpse must be carried for burial westward toward the great desert of Amenti, the abode of spirits, and must be carried over water. Where the Nile did not flow between a city and its cemetery an artificial lake was made. In this custom the classic myth of the Acherusian Lake originated.

The ground plan of the Memphian Necropolis suggests a huge dumb-bell, extending from north to south twenty miles, with an average breadth of two, the handle nearly as thick as the lobes, and bounded on the east by the Acherusian Lake, on the west by the desert. It was laid out in streets lined with tombs. Most of the tombs were one-storied houses of stone or marble, containing one or two apartments, which were decorated with mural paintings and sculptures, and furnished with all possible appliances of luxury and comfort. Even dolls for the dead little children were not forgotten. Beneath these chambers the mummies were laid in subterranean vaults, while the superior chambers were intended for the use of the disembodied spirits, and were much frequented by friends who sought in them communion with the departed. Only the rich were thus interred. The bodies of the poor were dipped in a chemical wash to retard decay, and thrust into the desert sand west of the City of the Dead.

The north lobe of the dumb-bell, lifted upon a ridge of limestone, is occupied by the great pyramids. It was approached from the east by a paved causeway, which terminated between the paws of the oldest and grandest idol in the world, the great Sphinx of the Nile. The fore-paws of the idol are of masonry; the rest of the figure is sculptured from the native rock. The lion's body, 172 feet in length, the woman's breasts, the man's face, still remain. Once a granite temple appeared between the fore limbs, sheltered in the bosom, and incense ascended day and night to the nostrils sixty feet above the altar. Upon the brows, which were a hundred feet in circumference, rested the royal helmet of Egypt, and from the chin drooped the royal beard. This emblem of eternity, rising from the margin of the desert to watch the Nile, guarded the northern entrance of the City of the Dead. Behind it the three great pyramids stood among a group of smaller ones like mountains among hills. One of them was red, one gray, the largest white. From a base which covered thirteen acres, a mass of solid stone rose to an apex 470 feet in air. Its sides were faced with slabs of pure white limestone polished, and so deftly joined that a sheet of paper could not be inserted between them. The structure represented the labor of seven million men.

To the south of this place of pyramids, in the handle of the dumb-bell, stood the temple of Serapis. It was the most unique edifice in Egypt, and may have suggested the catacombs at Rome.

During its lifetime the sacred bull was kept among the living in a temple on the east of the Acherusian Lake and worshiped as Apis. If it died before it was twenty-five years old,[1] it became Serapis. The body was embalmed, and lay in state for eighty

[1] Since M. Mariette found two of these bovine mummies which had lived twenty-six years, this qualification has seemed doubtful.

days, which the whole land passed in mourning. Then it was transported with imposing ceremonies, in which the king was prominent, across the lake for interment in the Serapeum. That portion of the temple which stood above ground has vanished, and its appearance can only be conjectured. But the important parts of the structure were subterranean and still remain. These are vast galleries hewn in the solid rock and opening at intervals of about fifty yards into high arched vaults. Each vault contains a huge sarcophagus of black polished marble cut from a single block, and so large that Dean Stanley says they seem more like chambers than coffins. M. Mariette has recently discovered another of these rock-hewn galleries two thousand feet long, lined on both sides with chambers occupied by similar sarcophagi. Each of these marble coffins contained the mummy of an Apis, and here from immemorial time until after the Christian era the sacred bulls were buried.

South from the Serapeum a second cluster of pyramids, inferior in size to the first but probably much older, marks the south lobe of the dumb-bell.

Excepting the Sphinx, the pyramids, and

the subterranean galleries of the Serapeum, this once magnificent Necropolis is now a chaos of sand heaps and shreds of mummy cloth, and fragments of stone, glass, pottery, for every foot of the space has been dug up many times by those destructive ragpickers of the East, Arabs searching for treasure.

On the edge of the depression once filled by the Acherusian Lake, a colossus of red granite, cut from a single block and weighing four hundred tons, lies half buried in the sand. The features are still distinct. The brows are broad, the forehead fine, the nose slightly aquiline. It is a handsome face of pure Caucasian type, and is an authentic portrait of the king " who knew not Joseph," and whose task-masters compelled the children of Israel to render the full tale of bricks when the supply of straw was refused them. The name of Ramses II. is inscribed upon the girdle. The same face is repeated upon the temple walls of upper Egypt; in the colossi which line the approach to the Temple of Thebes, and in the report of the Egypt Exploration Fund for 1883–84, M. Petrie describes a statue of the same king, fragments of which have been found at Tanis, the ancient Zoan, and which he estimates to have been ninety feet in height and in weight nine hundred tons. For a considerable period the chief industry of Egypt appears to have been the manufacture of pictures and statues of this king. Our Bibles tell us that when the children of Israel asked for mercy their oppressors replied : " Ye are idle ! ye are idle ! Therefore ye say let us go ! " A sepulchral fresco earlier than Ramses II. shows in colors which are still vivid an overseer among slaves in a brickyard holding a whip and saying, in words inscribed beneath : " The rod is in my hand, be not idle ! Be not idle ! "

We may pause to note a few of many illuminations which Egyptologists have cast upon the Scriptures. It puzzles children to understand why all the kings of Egypt had the same name, until they are told that Pharaoh was the royal title and meant " Great House," as " Sublime Porte " or " great gate " is the title of Turkish monarchs. Older people have wondered to hear Joseph say that God had made him " a father to Pharaoh," and been relieved to learn that the Hebrew word for father was identical in sound with the Egyptian word for " prime-minister." And scholars were gratified when Dr. Brugsch proved that the unintelligible name given to Joseph by Pharaoh, Zaphnath-paaneah, which had so long glared at them in Genesis xli. 45, was the title of the governor of the district over which Joseph ruled, and signified " the ruler of the district where dwells the Living One," that is, " the home of Jehovah." M. Naville has proved that the district called by that name was the Goshen assigned to the Israelites, and we read in Exodus that God revealed himself to Moses by his new name, " the Living One."

The mummy of Ramses II., the Pharaoh of the oppression, has been found and identified by Prof. Maspero. The mummy of his favorite son, wearing a mask of gold and wrapped in cloths written over with repetitions of his name, has also been discovered in the Serapeum. No other Egyptian king is so well-known as Ramses II.

Egypt produced no military genius who can be ranked among the world's great captains. Thotmes III. was the ablest of her warriors, but Ramses II. was the most famous. Before he was twelve years old his father Sethos made him associate king. Some have supposed that he was the Sesostris of

Herodotus. It has been conjectured that the blended names of father and son, Sethos-Ramses, softened into Sesostramsis, Sesostris, may have given rise to the name by which he was known to the Greeks.

He was the vainest of men. He multiplied statues of himself beyond all count, and erected temples and monuments to cover them with his portraits and the records of his achievements. Never was monarch so well advertised. He was fortunate in having a poet laureate named Pentaur, the Homer of the Nile, to sing his praises. The most important composition of this bard is a poem, which won the prize in a national competition, and may be called the Ramsiad for the same reason which has named the Odyssey. It is much older than the Iliad, and relates the exploits of Ramses in a campaign against the people of Khita. The poem exists on papyrus, and entire walls of temples at Abydos, Luknor, Karnak, and Ipsamboul are inscribed with its verses, or adorned with illustrations of the scenes it describes. The colors of the pictures are fresh and vivid.

One shows the king in camp. The camp is a square, intrenched with a foss and an embankment along which the shields of the soldiers are placed in line for a breastwork. In the centre, beside a movable shrine of the deity, is the king, and at his feet crouches his favorite lion, named "Smarkaftor," or "The Destroyer." An inscription explains that this is the camp of the legion, named "The Bestower of Victory upon Ramses Miamun." It was probably his body-guard.

A second picture represents two foreigners dragged in chains before the king. Egyptians are beating and pushing them forward. The inscription reads: "This is the arrival of two spies of the people of Khita. They are beating them to make them tell where the king of Khita is."

Who were the people of Khita? A very few years ago the question could not have been answered.

When astronomers noticed that the planets appeared to disobey the laws of gravity, they began to search for the cause of the disturbance and discovered a new star. A similar experience led to the discovery of the people of Khita.

When ancient history began to be critically studied, the known forces appeared inadequate to account for all the phenomena which came to view. The vast armaments of Egypt and Assyria were seen to have received checks from some unknown source or sources. It had been long observed that the Bible speaks of the Hittites in a way which seems inappropriate to a tribe so small and weak as that people were supposed to have been. There was also a vivid Greek tradition of warrior women called Amazons, who had lived somewhere in the east of Asia Minor. The excavations of Dr. Schliemann brought to light obvious traces of an artistic influence which could not be adequately explained by reference to any source previously known, but which must also have come from eastern Asia Minor. Further still, certain rock sculptures had been observed from very early times in the region to which these several indications pointed. The Greeks had attributed them to the Egyptians, for the Greeks habitually referred to the Egyptians all great works which they could not claim as their own.

The best known of these sculptures was that of a colossal warrior carved in relief upon the face of a cliff near Sardes. Herodotus saw it, and said it was carved by Sesostris. For twenty-four centuries the statement passed unquestioned. But as scholars grew critical they began to wonder why these figures on the rocks of Asia Minor wore boots with pointed toes such as were never seen in Egypt, but precisely similar to those still used by the mountaineers of the Taurus, and resembling those which appear upon the feet of Xerxes in the sculptured relief of that monarch as he sat at Susa. Neither the costumes nor the faces of these mysterious figures are Egyptian. Fifty miles east of the Halys a bas-relief was found which represents a procession of male and female figures. The male figures wear Phrygian caps, but the female mural crowns. The inscriptions accompanying these sculptures are cut in relief, while Egyptians almost invariably cut in intaglio. More than sixty such inscriptions have come to light, and though they have not yet been deciphered, they are obviously neither Egyptian nor Assyrian, nor Hebrew nor Greek, nor any other language known to living scholars. Similar inscriptions were found at Carchemish on the Euphrates.

The great Egyptian picture at Ipsamboul contains 1,100 figures. It represents a battle between Ramses II. and the king of Khita. The people of Khita depicted in it are in face and costume precisely like those sculptured upon the rocks of Asia Minor. Eventually a bilingual inscription in cuneiform and the unknown tongue was fortunately found, which confirmed the growing suspicions and completed the proof that there had been in eastern Asia Minor a powerful nation contemporary with the great monarchies of Egypt and Assyria and able to cope with them on equal terms. The existence of this people had not been suspected. One of their capitals was Carchemish on the Euphrates, the other Kadesh on the Orontes. They worshiped Istar, the Babylonian Bellona. She was served by women. Kadesh — the same root as Cadiz — implies the abode of "Holy women," and her priestesses armed and marching first in processions gave rise to the Greek tradition of the Amazons. Defeated by Sargon at Carchemish B. C. 717, this nation vanished from history so completely that a few years ago no man suspected that it had existed. Scholars are waiting for new discoveries to teach them more of this mysterious race. They must have been to some extent a literary people, for the Bible tells us they had founded in the south of Palestine, "Kirjiath-Sepher," or "Book-town," and dwelt there in the time of Joshua, and their inscriptions are finely cut.

It was against this people — the Hittites or children of Heth, whose daughters were detested by Rebecca and loved by Solomon, from whose sons Abraham purchased his burial-place and David stole a wife, by murdering her husband — that Ramses II. waged the war described in Pentaur's poem.

The descriptions of the Egyptian poet read as if they had been written by Homer in his dotage. Ramses is made to relate his own achievements. The crisis of the narrative appears when the king had fallen into an ambush, and been separated from his army. "Then," exclaims the modest hero, "I became like the God Menu. I hurled the dart with my right hand. I fought with my left hand. I was like Baal to their sight. I had come upon 2,500 pairs of horses. I was in the midst of them, but they were dashed in pieces before my steeds. Their courage sank, their limbs gave way; they could not hurl the dart; they could not wield the spear." The boaster proceeds to tell how he drove his favorite war-horse named "Victory for Thebes," dashing hither and thither at will; seizing iron-clad heroes in his hands and hurling them into the Orontes. It is not difficult to see why Pentaur's poem won the prize. Although Ramses's victory is represented as complete, it appears that he carried home no spoils, and was glad to conclude a peace with the king of Khita. The terms of the treaty, first inscribed upon a silver disk, are repeated upon the temple walls at Karnak, and have been translated into English. Ramses married afterwards a daughter of the Hittite king, and it is possible that she was the mother of the princess who educated Moses.

The later wars of Ramses were only organized man-hunts, prosecuted to secure slaves for the great works he executed. Among those works were temples at Luxor, Ipsamboul, and Memphis, and most significant of them all to us, the treasure cities to construct which the Hebrews toiled. These were located on the east of the Nile Delta as fortresses to guard the Eastern Gate of Egypt, and as granaries for military supplies. The site of Ramses (Exodus i. 11) is still uncertain. That of Pithom has been fixed by the excavations of M. Naville as Tell el Maskutah, or "The Mound of the

Statue," so named from a monolith of red granite representing Ramses II. seated in an armchair between the two solar gods Ra and Tum. Enormous chambers, inclosed by brick walls six and twelve feet thick and designed for the storing of grain, have there been found.

In the construction of these " treasure cities " the children of Israel toiled until oppression drove them to flight.

In the reign of Manephta II., the son and successor of Ramses, a coalition of enemies invaded Egypt. The invasion was repelled, but not until it had so greatly weakened Egypt that the Israelites were able to effect their escape.

The religion of Egypt moulded her history. It began with a lofty conception of the unity of God, and its earliest literature expresses an ethical spirit which will at times bear comparison with the psalms of David. It ended in a polytheism the most extravagant and abject. It appealed solely to motives drawn from the hope of reward or the fear of punishment after death. Its failure seems to have led Moses to reject altogether appeals to the life to come while he emphasized with all his force the pleasures and the pains of the life that now is. The conspicuous and disastrous breakdown of the religion of Egypt teaches a lesson which was repeated with terrible distinctness in the history of the monks of Alexandria, that neither a religion of fear nor a religion of hope, but only the religion of love, can save a people from their sins.

V.

ALEXANDRIA, THE CITY OF THE CREED MAKERS.

FOUNDED by the greatest warrior of Greece, betrayed to the greatest warrior of Rome by the most bewitching woman of antiquity, and destroyed by the ablest of the early Saracen conquerors, Alexandria was for a considerable time the first city in the world, and then took rank as second. It was the gate to the chief granary of the Roman Empire; the hot-bed in which modern European literatures and sciences were rooted; the intellectual workshop where were forged those pagan creeds which resisted Christianity most successfully; the foundry where Judaism was melted, and remoulded into the last and most alluring of its many perverted forms, and the seminary where Christianity first received scientific statement in the dogma, which eighteen centuries have confirmed as the fundamental doctrine of the church.

Though rarely mentioned in the Bible, the influence of Alexandria pervades the New Testament as an atmosphere, unseen but omnipresent. Those oracles of our faith were written in a language finally prepared to receive them not at Athens, but at Alexandria, and differing from the Greek of Plato almost as much as the English of Shakespeare differs from that of Chaucer. The part of John's Gospel which affirms that " the Word was made flesh, and dwelt among us," is expressed in terms of the Alexandrian philosophy, and the version of the Old Testament largely used by the Apostles in their preaching was made at Alexandria.

The distinct allusions to Alexandria in the New Testament, though few, are full of interest.

It was the home of that " certain Jew " who probably wrote the epistle to the Hebrews, and whom Paul yoked with himself in the familiar utterance, " Paul may plant, and Apollos water." A synagogue of Alexandrians in Jerusalem had part in moving the Jews to stone Stephen, when Paul held the garments of the murderers, watched the face " become as the face of an angel," and heard the voice saying, " I see Jesus standing at the right hand of God." A ship of Alexandria carried the great Apostle to die at Rome, and Simon of Cyrene, more to be envied than Simon Peter on the greatest day of history, came from the west of Alexandria, and must almost certainly have passed through the streets of that city to reach the road over which he bore the Master's cross.

Mareotis was the largest of the many little lakes in the delta of the Nile. It was separated from the Mediterranean by a narrow limestone ridge some five miles long, and one in average breadth. This belt of land shaped in a flattened curve, thrust its east and west extremities north into the sea, like the flukes of an anchor. Midway between them was a small village named Rhacotis. In the sea, due north of the village, nearly a mile from land, lay a small and nameless island. The sheltered water between the village and the island, much frequented by Greek and Phœnician rovers, was called "Pirate's Bay." Here, 332 B. C., Alexander the Great planned the city which his general and successor built.

An enormous mole thrust from the village to the island completed the anchor by giving the arms a shank and stock. The two commodious harbors thus formed on the east and the west of the great mole were joined together by two broad canals spanned by drawbridges. On the northeast tip of the island a lighthouse of white stone four hundred feet high was erected, which ranked among the seven wonders of the world. It gave to the island its own name, Pharos or The Lighter.

The modern town of Alexandria is confined to the mole. Of the ancient city the mole was a small part. A street two hundred feet wide ran due south, threading the mole from Pharos Island to Lake Mareotis. It was crossed at right angles by another of equal width, which threaded the anchor's arms, and was probably carried by a drawbridge over the great canal connecting the Mediterranean in front with the lake behind the city. At their crossing these main streets swelled into an oval, adorned with flowers, fountains, and statues. The west fluke of the anchor contained the Necropolis, which terminated, before reaching the shank, in the section occupied by the Egyptian residents, and retained the name of the original village, Rhacotis. East of Rhacotis lay the royal quarter occupied by Greeks and called

Brucheum. The east fluke of the anchor was inhabited by the Jewish residents, who numbered at the accession of Nero more than fifty thousand. The population of the city in the days of its grandeur was about 600,000, half of them slaves.

The first Ptolemy, probably a half brother of Alexander the Great, was one of the ablest sovereigns who have ever lived. He realized that mind is the master force, and relied on intellect to make Alexandria great. He strove to win without wasting what his predecessors had wasted without winning, and succeeded so well that the surname given him by the Rhodians in gratitude for the assistance he rendered them was generally accepted as descriptive of his character, and he was called Ptolemy the Saviour. His son and successor, named Ptolemy Philadelphus either in irony because he murdered two of his brothers, or to emphasize the fact that in contempt of Greek and compliance with Egyptian manners he married his sister, continued his father's plans with an almost equal ability.

The native Egyptians were stupid and superstitious. To secure their loyalty the first Ptolemy erected, within their quarter

Rhacotis, nearly the most magnificent temple of its period, scarcely inferior to that of Jupiter in the Capitol, and called it the Serapeum. If we may trust Arab tradition, a solitary relic of its splendor still remains overlooking the site of the ancient city from an artificial mound to which it was removed by Diocletian. It has been called Pompey's Pillar, from a mistake in deciphering the inscription, though Pompey had no connection with it and did nothing memorable in Alexandria but die. The fluted shaft of polished red granite, with Corinthian base and capital, rising more than ninety-two feet, is said by Arab tradition to be one of the four hundred stately columns which adorned the Serapeum. Though the great temple resembled the Serapeum of Memphis only in name, the native priests were bribed to declare that all was as it should be, and the Egyptians were easily persuaded. To attract a still larger constituency the attributes of all the most popular idols in the world were gradually assigned to Serapis, and here originated that system of idolatry which, blending various forms of pagan worship into one, reached its consummation in the Pantheon.

There was also a superb library attached to the Serapeum for those who cared to read, and to flatter native patriotism a priest named Manetho was set to recording the glories of Egyptian history.

Directly east of Rhacotis lay the Greek quarter, called Brucheum. Here stood the palace of the Ptolemies, and later of the Cæsars. Near the shore of the east harbor, to decorate the imperial gardens, or possibly to commemorate the spot where, in a golden coffin, Alexander's body, brought from Memphis, had been buried, Augustus placed the two obelisks known as Cleopatra's needles, which originally formed parts of the temple at Heliopolis, where the father-in-law of Joseph once ministered as priest. One of them now stands on the Thames embankment, the other in Central Park.

The most celebrated structure in the Brucheum or in Alexandria was the Museum.

Educated Greeks had ceased to reverence the gods of Olympus. Literature, science, and philosophy had taken the place of religion. But the Greeks were still the world's mind, and to win them was to rule the world, not by authority, but by influence. Aware of this, the Ptolemies founded and fostered "The Museum." It was an immense university, lavishly furnished with all that could attract intellectual men. It contained museums of natural history, botanical and zoölogical gardens, observatories, lecture halls, and a library which has had no peer until very recent times. Neither cost nor labor was spared to make this institution the thought-centre of the world. When originals could not be obtained, copies were procured of all known literary productions. To the zeal of the Ptolemies we are chiefly indebted for the preservation of so much Greek literature as has come down to us.

Fearful that Pergamus — which had been raised to eminence by another of Alexander's generals — might become a successful literary rival of Alexandria, a Ptolemy prohibited the exportation from Egypt of papyrus, the paper of the old world. In self-defense the Pergamites invented a preparation of sheepskin, suitable for writing, which was called after them, pergamite, or as gradually softened in pronunciation, parchment, and the words paper and parchment still preserve the history of this ancient strife for literary precedence.

To the Museum Ptolemy drew Euclid, who laid the basis of modern mathematics. It was he who, when asked by the king to make his geometry easier, replied that there was no royal road to learning. Here Archimedes, the father of modern mechanics, was educated. Here, too, Eratosthenes, who measured the obliquity of the ecliptic and estimated the circumference of the earth at 31,000 miles, pursued his studies. Here, too, Hipparchus correctly calculated the precession of the equinoxes, and originated the system developed in a later age by the astronomer after whom it was named the Ptolemaic, which, Mr. Kingsley says, though false in one assumption, was right in its method, and therefore served so long and so well.

Continuously, poets, artists, philosophers, and men of science, united in making the court of the Ptolemies the intellectual centre of the world. Alexandria absorbed the intellectual activity of her age, and became first, with scarcely a second. She originated almost nothing, except in mathematics, and even in that department discovered little which, though perhaps it had been forgotten, had not been elsewhere known before her day. But the gold of literature and science mined in earlier ages was carried to Alexandria, and there minted into current coin.

East of the Brucheum lay the Jewish quarter. In no single point of their administration did the two first Ptolemies display a keener statesmanship than in their treatment of that people. The only direction whence invasion need be feared was the east. Assailants from thence must traverse Palestine before reaching Egypt. Centuries had proved the hardihood of the Jews. Ptolemy Soter himself in fighting them by stealth bore witness to their valor. To win their friendship was to padlock the one unguarded door of his dominions.

Aware of this, he encouraged them to build a synagogue in Alexandria, flattered their vanity by feigning for their religion a respect he did not feel, granted them privileges they had received in no other land, pretended even to worship their Jehovah, sent for those rabbis who were scarcely willing to compass sea and land to make one proselyte and asked them to instruct him in their laws, requested them to translate their Scriptures into Greek for his great library, and so allured them in large numbers to his capital. The translation of the Old Testament, executed under the Ptolemies, is known as the Septuagint. It was the first ever made into a Gentile tongue, and was the version used by the great majority of readers in the time of Christ, when Hebrew had become a dead language even in Palestine. It is the version from which the Apostles frequently quote, and was the version used by the early Christians as the basis of other translations.

Ptolemy himself cared little for religion of any kind, but the skill with which he weaved the religious sentiments of others into the fabric of his own designs has never been surpassed, and rarely equaled. For two centuries Alexandria, under the Ptolemies, continued the most brilliant and influential city of the period. But the characters of her rulers steadily deteriorated. The last king of the illustrious dynasty, called in derision "The Flutist," deserved and received the contempt of his subjects. They refused to recognize the sovereignty of the daughter to whom, with her brother, he bequeathed his throne.

That daughter, Cleopatra, must be counted

one of the most fascinating women who has ever lived. Destitute of heart and destitute of conscience ; with no weapons but her beauty, her wit, and the marvelous melody of a voice which spoke seven languages, each as a mother tongue, three times she matched her single strength against the most powerful men in the world. Twice she conquered, once she failed ; and when that Cæsar Augustus from whom, Luke informs us, a decree went forth "that all the world should be taxed," effectually resisted her enchantments, surprise and indignation drove her to suicide. It is worth noting that the Cæsar whose government in Egypt protected the mother of Christ was the Cæsar whose fidelity to duty caused Cleopatra's death.

When scarcely eighteen, driven from her throne, at peril of her life she entered by a stratagem the private apartments of Julius Cæsar, who had come to Alexandria to be her judge. Mr. Froude counts Julius Cæsar the strongest man known to history. Cleopatra, in a single interview, bound the strong man, and held him in her fascinations until the dagger of Brutus ended at once his bondage and his life.

After Cæsar's death Mark Antony was

for a time the most powerful man in the world. Possibly angry with the dark-eyed queen, but more probably haunted by the recollection of her beauty and wishing to gaze on it again, he summoned her before him to answer the charge of having failed to use her influence against Cæsar's murderers. She came to him; not as a culprit; not as a suppliant; but as Venus Victrix. Gliding over the waters of the Cydnus in a gilded barge propelled by purple sails and oars of silver which kept time to the music of flutes; reclining beneath a golden canopy, with lovely children as cupids clustering around her, while fair women draped as graces handled the ropes and scattered perfumes in the air, she entered the public square of Tarsus, smiled in the face of the mighty warrior who had summoned her before him, and took him a willing captive with her jeweled hand. Thenceforth the great Triumvir followed her as an ox that is led to the slaughter, until in Alexandria he perished at her feet, having flung away a world for the kisses of the sorceress.

Cleopatra had made the court life of Alexandria a continuous revel of unspeakable debaucheries. The idolatries and superstitions of the whole world had intrenched themselves in the Serapeum. The philosophic culture of the Brucheum, severed from the court, was fast developing into systems similar to the Mesmerisms and Spiritisms of modern times. The Jews of Alexandria, flattered into a fierce and immoral conceit, had already helped to inoculate Jerusalem with the spirit which crucified Christ, when a new element, Christianity, entered the city. The Jews, the philosophic Greeks, the idolaters, and the court agreed in one respect. Each party despised and detested the others with equal intensity. Neither faction was destitute of good men. But their numbers were few. The immense majority was composed of fierce fanatics and sumptuous debauchees. The city became a hot-bed of riots. It was moving surely toward that condition which made it possible for the quarrel of a soldier and a townsman about a pair of shoes to inaugurate a conflict in which for twelve years the city was divided into three hostile camps, each protected by military fortifications from the other two, and making war upon them as it could. Alexandria had already become a witches' cauldron, where conflicting superstitions, creeds, and passions, stirred by the infernal powers, were boiling fiercely, when Christianity was cast into the hell-broth. It excited a still more furious strife. For some centuries Alexandria was a chief battle ground of the Church with the pagan world. During that period some of the best and wisest men known to Christian biography lived and worked there. Pantænus, Origen, Athanasius, deserve to rank almost with the Apostles. Their influence has come down the ages in perpetual benediction. But the mass of Christians in Alexandria were very ignorant and very superstitious. Goaded by persecution, and still more by the idolatries and debaucheries continually before their eyes, they assumed a fanaticism fiercer than that of pagan or Jew. But while recalling the sad facts we ought not to forget that the passion displayed by the monks in Alexandria was in a real sense and great degree a passion for righteousness. A passion provoked in part, it is true, by the persecutions they had endured, but still more by the sight of such orgies of sin as can scarcely in our day be conceived, — orgies in which a Roman senator in the theatre, painted as a sea god, had danced naked before the people, and crawled about the stage dragging a scaly tail, to imitate the dragons of mythology. It should not be forgotten that the fierce fanaticism of the Egyptian ascetics, like that of Cromwell's soldiers, was rarely used to win either profit or pleasure for themselves. Of those who defiled Alexandria with deeds which may perhaps be palliated, though they cannot be excused, some spent their nights in vigils and their days in fastings, and perpetrated cruelties in the name of Christ because they believed that only so could they keep their souls from being tortured in the fires of hell forever.

When the Emperor Theodosius issued the decree prohibiting idolatry throughout the Roman Empire, the archbishop of Alexandria welcomed his opportunity. That archbishop, Theophilus, was a fierce, bold, and cruel man. Alexandria was a magazine of gunpowder. Hints of suppressing the worship of Serapis were sparks. Theophilus took pains to scatter them. The pagans flew to arms. They intrenched themselves in the Serapeum. The Christians hastened to attack it. The temple was besieged. Prisoners taken in sallies by the idolaters were inhumanly tortured and immolated before the altars by its defenders. The streets of Rhacotis ran blood.

A truce was at last arranged until the Emperor's will could be learned. Each party expected a favorable reply from Theodosius, when they met on the public square to hear the message from Rome. The Christians raised a shout of triumph, for it decreed the destruction of the Serapeum. The idolaters fled and sought safety in concealment.

The Christians rushed upon the temple and began its demolition unresisted. But they paused in their ruthless work before the statue of Serapis. It was a colossal seated image, embodying the attributes of the most venerated deities of both Egypt and Greece. Its extended hands touched both walls of the sanctuary. It was made of plates of various metals inlaid with precious stones. The symbol of plenty, a golden basket, rested upon its head; a serpent, the emblem of eternity, coiled around its body and a three-headed cerberus crouched by its side. Many supposed it had been worshiped by the great Sesostris. The pagans believed that if this idol were overthrown the earth would open and swallow the city, or the sea rise and overwhelm it. The Christians were not free from similar apprehensions. They paused before the image in anxious suspense. In vain Theophilus strove by mocking taunts to urge them forward. A solitary Roman soldier, bearing a ladder and a battle-axe, advanced into the open space which superstitious fears had kept inviolate. No one ventured to assist him. As he laid the ladder upon the idol's shoulder and ascended its rounds, the Christians were spellbound by an awe they could not master. That soldier deserves to rank among the bravest of men. With all his force he struck his battle-axe into the idol's cheek. The golden plate fell crashing upon the stone pavement. That clang rang the loudest death-knell of idolatry in the Empire. The earth did not open, the sea did not rise. Frenzy again seized the Christians. Beneath repeated strokes the image fell. Awe swiftly changed to ridicule as a colony of mice, which had been sheltered in its body, appeared, scampering in terror away from their divine protector.

The Christians continued the work of destruction. They tore in fragments the precious contents of the library. They stripped the Serapeum of all that could be removed; they destroyed all that could be destroyed; and though baffled for a time by the stupendous strength of the structure, they did not rest until its stately columns had been broken, and built into a breakwater against the sea.

But the murder of Hypatia, in 415 A. D., is the darkest stain upon the religion of Alexandria. She was a heathen maiden, raised up, we may believe, to prove what Cleopatra had once made it hard to believe, that God does not leave Himself without a witness among any people. She was as true as Cleopatra was false, as gracious as Cleopatra was cruel, and though her beauty differed from that of Cleopatra, as a star hanging in the blue differs from a star shot from a Roman candle, perhaps she was as beautiful. Her genius drew crowds of honest seekers after truth to the museum when each day she expounded Plato, and strove nobly in the hopeless endeavor to regenerate society without Christ. Christian youths attended her lectures, and were ennobled by them. This was enough to convince the monks of Cyril that she was a sorceress sent by the devil to allure Christ's lambs to hell.

Slanders, to the effect that she had prejudiced the prefect of the city against the archbishop, circulated among the Christians, increased their rage against her.

They lay in wait for her in the street before the Museum. They tore her from her chariot. They dragged her to the church, called Cæsareum. They stripped off her clothing, rent her body limb from limb, cast the quivering flesh into the flame kindled in the public square, and so sent her spirit to tell the Master how his disciples had dealt with one who, in the best way she knew, was trying to do in Alexandria what the same demoniac zeal for a fiction they called God had crucified Him for doing in Jerusalem.

The same sectarian spirit which had long before destroyed Jerusalem caused the final ruin of Alexandria. Six hundred and thirty-eight years after Christ, the Christians in Egypt were quarreling over a quibble of doctrine of which they were not able to understand, and of which no one now need care to know, more than this: that one denomination called themselves Melchites, while the other called themselves Jacobites; and the essential creed of both was to hate one another with all their heart and mind and strength. In the crisis of this quarrel the Saracens invaded Egypt. Their advance was facilitated by the treachery of one of the Christian factions which had been driven by the other from Alexandria, and hoped to gain the upper hand by help of the common enemy. The city resisted in a siege of fourteen months. The Saracens attacked with vigor. Amrou their great commander, carried beyond his lines by his own impetuosity, with a single slave attending him, was taken prisoner. The Alexandrians did not recognize him. How should such drivelers recognize a hero? But as he was brought before the Christian prefect, the dignity of Amrou's bearing had nearly betrayed his identity even to them, when his quick-witted slave smote him upon the mouth, and bade him mind his manners in the presence of his betters. The Christians were completely deceived. They sent their illustrious captive back to negotiate a peace with the general who was himself. Is it not the irony of history that this city of creed-makers should have perished through adopting a false creed, not about the personality of God which they could not understand, but about the person of a man which they might easily have known?

Amrou again at the head of his army captured the city. At first he designed to preserve it uninjured, and carefully refrained from pillage. Four years later, provoked by the repeated attacks of the Romans, he decided upon its destruction. Its magnificence devastated, its library destroyed, its defenses thrown down, its harbor impaired, the skeleton alone remains to warn us that whenever we are tempted to think more of the letter, even of the Scriptures, than of the spirit which inspired them, we may read with profit a chapter from the history of Alexandria.

VI.

PETRA, THE CITY OF SHAMS.

The deep and dreary valley extending south a hundred and twenty miles from the Dead Sea to the eastern arm of the Red Sea was named from its extreme desolation "The Arabah," or "Waste." It is separated from the Arabian desert on the east by a belt of mountain twenty miles in average breadth. These mountains of porphyry capped with sandstone form a region of sharp needles, abrupt precipices, and wild gorges, threaded with fertile valleys and dotted with nests of rich ground. Westward it faces the Arabah valley in cliffs and rugged ascents, divided by savage chasms. Eastward it slopes more gently in striations of alternating ridge and hollow, and, though higher, the mountains are less barren as they drop downward toward the desert. Lofty peaks, attracting vapors from the Mediterranean Sea and the Indian Ocean, distribute a rainfall sufficient to create fertility wherever there is soil. The desert heat, tempered by the elevation and abundant moisture, renders the climate delightful.

This rugged territory is Mount Seir. By the Old Testament writers it was also called Edom, by the Greeks Idumæa. Petra was from immemorial time its most important city, though not continuously its capital. Petra is the Greek translation of the earlier name "Selah," the "Rock," and the rocky region lying east of the Arabah was in that tongue called Arabia Petræa, not because it was rocky, but because its capital was Petra.

Near the close of the last century the French traveler Volney, while encamped near Jericho, heard reports of remarkable ruins somewhere in the mountains of Idumæa. Fear of hostile Arabs deterred him from attempting to discover them. In 1812 Burckhardt, the Columbus of modern Oriental travel, undertook the task. He was master of the Arabic language, and familiar with Arabian manners. He wore the rags which constitute the average Bedouin toilet, and easily passed for one of the faithful upon a pilgrimage to Mecca. He gave out that a vow required him to sacrifice a goat at some sacred spot in the region he wished to explore, and the superstition of the natives guarantied his safety. Striking into the mountains a little south of the Dead Sea, he moved southeast by south some sixty miles, and entered a small valley near the edge of the desert. A stream crossed the valley and vanished in the wall of rock which rimmed the place on all sides but the east. Rounding a bulge in the precipice the traveler discerned a fissure cleaving it from base to summit. The Arabs called it the Sik or Cleft, and said it had been made by the rod of Moses. Into this fissure Burckhardt followed the stream. The chasm was scarcely more than twelve feet wide, and its walls were perpendicular. The stream had obviously been once confined within an artificial channel. A roadway broad enough for camels was paved with blocks of stone. There was sufficient earth to fringe with scarlet oleanders the path which sloped evenly downward. The fissure varied in width, as he advanced, from twelve to forty feet. Ferns grew from crevices in the walls. Trailing creepers hung festoons upon them. A bridge spanned the chasm near its entrance. A second glance showed it to be a triumphal arch. Beneath it niches cut for statues and framed between ornamental pilasters gave a weird effect to the deserted gallery. The traveler had advanced a mile along what seemed the enchanted entrance to some fairy land, when the chasm broadened and debouched into another running nearly at right angles to its course. It was morning and the open space was flooded with sunlight. Directly before him, hewn in the face of the cliff, stood a temple. Its Corinthian columns, richly ornamented, supported a pediment on which appeared a colossal stone eagle as if about to fly forth. The entrance beneath was guarded by equestrian sculptures, and above the portico, flanked by columnar towers resembling mimic temples, an "insulated cylinder" supported an enormous urn, which the Arabs said was filled with treasures placed there by Egyptian kings. The whole amazing structure glowed deep rose-color in the morning light, and the sunbeams reflected from behind the columns of the portico gave to parts of it the pink of an ocean shell. From the urn, conspicuous above all other parts of the temple, it is called the Khazné or Treasury.

I have called this structure a temple, and such from without it appears to be. The interior, a few paltry apartments twenty and thirty feet square, mocks such pretensions.

From this place of enchantment the gorge elbows sharply to the northwest, narrowing immediately to its former dimensions, and continues for a mile impressive as before. Then the right wall continuing straight on, the left wall bending backward, the fissure expands into an undulating plain several miles in circumference, inclosed on the east and west between precipices from three hundred to one thousand feet high, and shut in north and south by rugged sandstone mountains.

At the left hand of the gorge, at the point where it debouches into the open inclosure, stands a theatre, cut in the rock. The tiers, thirty-five in number, face from the plain. "Boxes" cut in the mountain open upon the broad corridor which circles behind and above the highest tier. The theatre will seat thirty-five hundred spectators, and is in such perfect preservation, says Stevens, "that if the bodies buried in the adjacent cliffs could come to life they might take their old places and listen to the declamations of their favorite players."

Here we will take our seat near by the city. On our right the precipice continues northward, nearly a mile. Its face is honeycombed with dwellings or tombs. Which to call them no man knows. Some of them are plain, some are adorned with façades like Grecian temples. They open upon different levels, and must have been reached by approaches cut in the face of the rock. Opposite this wall of cliff, west across the plain, another like it shows the same surprising cuttings. The mountains which bound the plain upon the north are also filled with them. The south boundary slopes upward in more gradual ascents.

The stream along which Burckhardt entered bisects the plain from east to west, and disappears in a chasm which has not been explored. The city of Petra stood upon the plain on both sides of the stream. The site is covered with ruins, among which a Roman arch of triumph and a citadel are still distinct. The purpose of the cliff cuttings which surround the city and fill the sides of gorges opening into it is not known. They are innumerable and represent incredible labor. Some think that they were tombs, some that they were dwellings; others that they were an intermixture of both. A plausible theory infers that they were designed solely as ornaments. For a time the whole commerce of the East paid tribute to Petra, and it has been supposed that the citizens, possessing enormous wealth, and unable to adorn their suburbs in any other way, took this means of gratifying their love of beauty. There is probably some truth in each hypothesis. The primitive Horites or cave-dwellers named in Genesis probably dwelt in the cliffs. When the city on the plain was founded they may have gradually removed to it, and used the caves for sepulchres. The Idumæans supplanted the Horites. When the Nabathæans took possession of the place three centuries before Christ the age of its splendor began. Shut in by a wall of rock from every breeze, the citizens would naturally seek relief from the heat of summer in the surrounding elevations, where alone it could be found. In time the superb carvings were made to adorn retreats in which the rich sought for coolness and repose. Whatever else future explorations may disclose, one fact is certain: The splendor of these mysterious structures was wholly on the outside. Within they were pitiful hovels. This is among the reasons which justify our calling Petra the city of shams.

On a summit near the city a watch-tower still remains. A line of similar towers has been traced northward nearly to Hebron. These watch-towers of Idumæa are most interesting to us as the objects in Isaiah's mind when he wrote the words rendered in the favorite hymn, "Watchman, tell us of the night." It may also be that Balaam stood upon such an one within the horizon of Bethlehem when he uttered the prediction: "I shall see Him, but not now: I shall behold Him, but not nigh: there shall come a star out of Jacob, and a sceptre shall rise out of Israel."

Hard by Petra stands Mount Hor. It rises five thousand feet above the Arabah, in three circular terraces of sandstone, and marks one of the few localities in the journey of the children of Israel about the identity of which there is no reasonable doubt. For unknown reasons it has been from prehistoric times regarded as a sacred spot. At the base of this mountain Moses halted, after nearly forty years of wandering. He had asked from the king of Edom permission to pass east around Moab through his dominions. The messengers had returned when Moses took Aaron, and Eleazar his son, and went up into the mountain in the sight of all the congregation. And Moses stripped Aaron of his priestly garments and put them upon Eleazar his son; and Aaron died there in the top of the mountain. And Moses and Eleazar came down from the mount. And all Israel mourned thirty days for Aaron.

The Idumæan king fiercely refused to allow the Israelites a passage through his territory. They were forced to retrace their steps south to the Red Sea. It was a weary journey, heavy with the sand driven north from the Gulf of Akabah. Travelers tell us it is infested with sand-colored snakes, small, but venomous, which escape notice on account of their color. The Bible tells us that here the Israelites, tantalized perhaps by the sight of orchards and vineyards they had seen but not entered, began to loathe their simple fare. "They murmured," and "the Lord sent serpents among them," which bit them, "and thousands died." Then Moses lifted up before their eyes that brazen serpent, the mysterious sign of healing throughout the ancient world, to which the Master referred when He strove to make men recognize in Him the Good Physician.

The Idumæans were the bitterest and most persistent enemies Israel ever had. Family feuds are proverbially implacable, and Esau was the twin brother of Jacob. The Edomites fiercely refused the reasonable request of Moses. When Nebuchadnezzar invaded Judah they rushed to his assistance. When Nehemiah began to build the temple they were there to hinder him. In describing the final triumph of Israel, and the destruction of her enemies, Isaiah included all her foes in the one representative name of Edom, and pictured Jehovah returning from the devastation of that land, as welcomed by the triumphal salutation, "Who is this that cometh from Edom!"

More than a century and a half before Christ, the Idumæans, who had been driven from Petra north toward the southern boundaries of Judah, were conquered by Judas Maccabæus, the greatest warrior of Israel after Joshua. After the death of Judas his nephew John Hyrcanus offered them the alternative of death or circumcision. They submitted, and thus made sham Jews they entered into a sham reconciliation, which continued with many breaks and bickerings for nearly a century.

The inevitable result of such feigned sentiments appeared in the animosities which seethed around the throne of Herod the Great.

That monarch, chiefly known to Bible readers by his murder of the innocents, hated by the Jews as a sham Jew, ridiculed by the Romans as a sham Roman, gibbeted in the question of the wise men as a sham king, was an Idumæan. His father had lived for a time at Petra, and was the intimate associate of the Arabian king. Herod also sought the alliance of the Arabians, though like most of his friends they became the subjects of his enmity the instant it appeared his interest to fight them. Though a bad, he was a bold man, and the campaign in which he won the admiration of the Romans shows traces of an experience gained among the caves of Edom.

A few miles west of the Sea of Galilee, in the gorge of Magdala, was a mimic Petra, named Arbela. Here caves cut in the cliff opened into galleries hewn along its face. Brigands were in possession of these strongholds. Amply provisioned, and supplied with water by cisterns sunk into the rock and filled by the rainfall, they resisted successfully even Roman skill and valor. Herod made iron crates, filled them with armed men, suspended them from the brow of the precipice by iron chains which could not be cut, and so was fought a strange battle between men hanging in the air and men intrenched in the solid rock. Herod gained the victory, and the bandits were exterminated.

By force, flattery, and lies combined he gained the Jewish throne. To please the Jews he built a temple to Jehovah on Mount Moriah. To please the Romans he inaugurated Greek and Roman games, and built a theatre in Jerusalem. In spite of these achievements he won the contempt of the Romans, and the detestation of the Jews. When he had murdered his wife and his two favorite sons at the instigation of a third, and the third son on the slander of a eunuch, at seventy years of age he was attacked by a disorder so painful that he attempted suicide, so offensive that no attendant could endure many moments of his presence. Foreseeing his death he summoned the elders of Israel to receive his last will at Jericho. There he kept them under strict guard in the hippodrome, and compelled his officers to swear that every man of them should be slain the instant he breathed his last, that there might be mourning at his funeral.

Thus perished the sham king which Petra helped inflict upon Israel.[1] He died six months after her true king had been born, and the joy of men over his loathsome funeral was exceeded only by the joy of angels over the birth of Christ. It was to men who for thirty-seven years had endured the oppressions of a monster who may truthfully be called the " destroyer," that the heralds sang, " Unto you is born this day a Saviour, which is Christ the Lord."

It is suggestive to remember that the same race which strove to check the advance of Moses, sent forth at last the sumptuous and energetic criminal who strove to murder in his cradle the Saviour of the world.

[1] By the alliance between Herod's father and the king of Petra, Antipater's "very familiar friend," by whose aid Antipater gained a controlling influence in Jerusalem. See Hausrath, vol. i. p. 208, Eng. trans., and Josephus, *Ant.* 14. 1. 4.

VII.

DAMASCUS, THE CITY OF SUBSTANCE.

I could wish to lead you to Damascus by a route which, though partially explored, has not, I think, been traversed. Leaving the Mediterranean some few miles north of Tyre, and striking inland a little north of east across a mile or two of fertile plain, we reach the range called "The White Mountains," or "Lebanon." East of it sinks the deep, rich valley named "The Syrian Hollow," or "Cœle Syria." Here distracted little brooks rush about in a bewildered manner, or pause in meditative pools, as if trying to determine whether they ought to go southwest with the Leontes for the benefit of Tyre, or south, to help the Jordan sweeten the Dead Sea, or east, in vain attempt to reach the Barada, and aid it in giving cups of cold water to the great thirsty desert. The range east of the valley is called "The White Mountain's Vis-à-Vis," or Antilebanon. This we cross at the highest point, which is named, from its dazzling snows, "The Glitterer," but is better known to us as Mount Hermon, or "The Lofty." Nine thousand feet of vigorous, and often dangerous climbing have brought us to its summit, three cones so ranged as to appear from east and west as one. Here a circle of huge stones, like the mysterious dolmens of western Europe, and the ruins of a temple belonging to a period comparatively recent, remind us that from before Abraham's day, until after Christ, Mount Hermon was a centre of Syrian sun-worship.

It is afternoon. Southward, amid the roots of the mountain, the Sea of Galilee glitters, like a bit of glass dropped in a bed of flowers. Westward, the Mediterranean glows, a sheet of burnished gold. Eastward, a black shadow is stealing down the mountain. It glides over the plain; it becomes the most marvelous of shadows, a slender cone of darkness stretching seventy miles across the desert, and stabbing the flushed sky till the sun sinks and the phantom vanishes in night. The bright speck gleaming in this cone of darkness a third of the distance toward its apex is Damascus. Its appearance is symbolic of its history, for, in the darkness which conceals all other cities of equal age, Damascus alone appears, old as Ur and young as Boston. We have come to view the city from a place whence we think the Master might have been seen when his face shone as the sun and his garments were white as the light. It was early morning then, and the shadow lay eastward upon the sea, while the transfigured Saviour talked with Moses and Elias concerning his decease, which he should accomplish at Jerusalem.

With solemn thoughts we descend the east side of the mountain. Sharp elevations shut us in until we reach the foot-hills and pause upon the spot whence the devout camel-driver gazed upon the city in which he now is worshiped, and exclaimed, "Man can have but one Paradise, and mine is above."

Five hundred feet below us lies the plain of the desert. Beside us the Barada, called by ancient Syrians "The Eternal," by Greeks "The Golden River," forcing its way through the mountain barrier, flows eastward more than twenty miles, till lost in three diminutive lakes which lie upon the sand like drops of dew upon a waste of ashes, or as if the finger of Lazarus had touched the tongue of Dives. United with a smaller stream by an incomparable system of irrigation, the river is made to fertilize every foot of ground for more than ten miles from both its banks. An oasis of exquisite verdure, threaded with silver and musical with rippling waters, extends from the roots of the barren mountains into the burning, silent waste. Here grows every flower that is pleasant to the eye, and every fruit that is good for man to eat.

> "And here are gardens bright with sinuous rills,
> Where blossoms many an incense-bearing tree,
> And here are forests, ancient as the hills,
> Enfolding sunny spots of greenery."

Two miles from the hill on which we stand, and separated from it by a lawn of turf like England's richest; surrounded by orchards of pomegranates, apricots, and olives; girt with a wealth of roses sufficient to supply the world with its most valued perfume; on the south bank of the Barada, but swelling across the stream in many a sunny suburb, the white domes and gilded minarets of Damascus gleam amid the foliage, or glitter above it beneath the soft Syrian sky. For five thousand years it has gleamed, an eye in the desert. It has never been a large city, nor a strong, nor a warlike, but rather one of the meek, to whom the inheritance of the earth is promised. Its days have been chiefly spent in feeding the hungry, clothing the naked, and doing good to those who have despitefully used and persecuted it. Whenever, as has occurred three or four times in five millenniums, its heart has been puffed up, and it has tried to exercise lordship over its brethren, some speedy check has stripped off its finery and sent it back to the better business, which has always been resumed with cheerful alacrity. A humble, hopeful, cheerful city, it is the bright speck in the deep shadow that lies upon the ancient world.

Though the oldest of cities, Damascus contains few ruins, for, like a thrifty housewife, it has continually made over its old garments into new raiment to suit the changing seasons; like nature, perpetually converting its rubbish into fresh forms of beauty, it has continually renewed its youth.

We will glance at the few features of the place which are known to have met the eyes of Paul : —

A triple arch spanning three gateways, and facing east and west. A mile due east of this, its duplicate. The two united by four parallel lines of white marble Corinthian columns. The inner colonnade of the three thus formed is roofed, and reserved for pedestrians. The outer two are open to the sky, and used by chariots. This triple colonnade, a mile in length, was the "street called Straight." Fancy it the string of a bow when strung, and the south wall of the city, at no point distant the quarter of a mile from the string, will represent the bow itself. The north wall completed a rectangle of which the bowstring was the south base, and the sides, extending northward to the river, were half a mile in length. These walls existed before the Roman period, and their course is still distinctly traceable. The city proper, the area within the walls, was considerably less than four hundred acres, but the overflow of suburbs varied in every age.

In the northwest angle of the walls, and near the river, stands "The Castle." It occupies one of the two sites in the ancient city which have been identified with certainty. A quadrangle flanked with towers, it was once a place of formidable strength, but is now a shell thin and weak with age.

The military recollections of Damascus naturally cluster around this fastness. David was the first recorded conqueror of the city. It regained its independence during the reign of Solomon, and though frequently captured and plundered in succeeding centuries by Egypt and Assyria, neither of those nations was able to hold it long in subjection because of the other.

It was probably a temporary repulse of the Assyrians, under Shalmaneser II., by the Dasmascene general Naaman to which reference is made in 2 Kings v. 1: "by him the Lord had given deliverance unto Syria." The statement was perplexing because the Scripture narrative gives no hint of any deliverance needed at that time by Syria, which had long had the upper hand of Israel. But when the boastful inscriptions of Shalmaneser, which record his three campaigns against Damascus, were deciphered, they made the statement plain. It was from Assyria that the Lord gave Damascus deliverance by the hand of Naaman.

"Now Naaman was a leper," and dear to every Christian child is the story of the "little maid brought away captive out of the land of Israel" who waited upon his wife, and said to her, "would God my lord was with the prophet that is in Samaria, for he would recover him of his leprosy," so that Naaman took $60,000 in gold and ten changes of raiment for a physician's fee, and was healed for nothing by Elisha.

More than a century later Pekah, the usurping king of Israel, conspired with Rezin, king of Damascus, to capture Jerusalem, dethrone its feeble monarch Ahaz, and put in his place their minion, "the son of Tabeal." The coalition appeared irresistible. The heart of Ahaz and the hearts of his people were moved "as the trees of the wood are moved by the wind" when it was told them "Syria is confederate with Ephraim." Isaiah, the greatest of ancient statesmen because the greatest of ancient seers, rebuked the general panic in the contemptuous exhortation: "Fear not the two tails of these smoking fire-brands," for their confederacy shall not stand. In less than a generation, he declared, the riches of Samaria and the spoils of Damascus should be taken away by the king of Assyria. Then lifting his eyes to broader horizons the seer uttered the great prediction, "Unto us a child is born, unto us a son is given, and the government shall be upon his shoulders, and his name shall be called Wonderful, Counsellor, the Mighty God, the Everlasting Father, the Prince of Peace. And of the increase of his government there shall be no end."

These three predictions were elicited by the same emergency. The first was fulfilled within the year. Assyrian inscriptions show that the second was accomplished by Tiglath-Pileser. If from Isaiah's race no child has yet been born, whom men have counted wonderful, whose counsel they have invoked in perplexity, whose aid they have sought in weakness, whom Christmas days have crowned the Prince of Peace; if no such child has yet been born, Isaiah's third prediction, uttered seven centuries before the birth of Christ, still waits for its fulfillment.

After the great conquerors of Egypt and Asia, each in his day, had captured and plundered Damascus, it was taken without resistance by Parmenio for Alexander the Great. In it Pompey spent the proudest year of his life, 64 B. C., distributing at his pleasure the thrones of the East to the vassals of Rome. Cleopatra had received the city as a love-gift from Mark Antony, and Tiberius had bestowed it upon Herod the Great, before Aretas of Petra, the father of the princess whom Herod Antipas divorced for Herodias' sake, and the ruler whose officers watched the city to prevent the escape of Paul, made it, we know not how, a part of his dominions.

We cannot follow the varying fortunes of Damascus from the age of Aretas to that of Heraclius. In 634 A. D. it was captured by the Saracens. A generation later it was made their capital, and for a time remained at the head of an empire which extended from the Atlantic to beyond the Tigris.

Some centuries later Noureddin established a system of communication never equaled before the electric telegraph, by which carrier pigeons flew at regular intervals from posts in his dominions, bearing letters beneath their wings, to their cotes in the gardens of Damascus.

The body of Noureddin's successor, Saladin, the only man who could match English Cœur de Leon in personal encounter, lies near the great mosque. It is he of whom the somewhat doubtful story is related, that when death drew nigh he ordered his favorite war horse, bearing his arms and his shroud, to be led along the "street called Straight" by a herald crying, "This is all that remains of Saladin the Great."

One more glance at the castle in the year 1401 A. D. shows the quadrangle filled with corpses. They are the corpses of its brave defenders. Tamerlane stands among them. He has received a ransom of fifty millions for their lives, pledged his honor for their safety, slaughtered them in cold blood, to a man, and after an indiscriminate massacre of the rest of her inhabitants he will reduce Damascus to ashes, and depart to build upon the ruins of Bagdad his pyramid of 90,000 human heads.

A little east of the castle stands the great mosque of Damascus. On the site it covers stood, most probably, in the age of Abraham, a temple to the sun. Here, too, it has been plausibly inferred, Naaman bowed by Elisha's permission while his master leaned upon him to worship Rimmon, and hence came the pattern of the altar which Ahaz copied in Jerusalem; for here, Mr. Porter strongly inclines to think, was the centre of those abominations from which, in the time of Paul, a majority of the women of Damascus sought shelter in Judaism. In the great mosque traces still remain of Christian by the side of Saracenic architecture. Beneath it the head of John the Baptist was said to have been laid, inclosed in a golden casket. When the Saracens took the city in 634 they entered simultaneously the opposite gates of the "street called Straight." One party entered by assault, the other by surrender. Neither knew that the other had passed the barrier until they met near the centre of the city at St. Mary's church. The leader of the fighting band insisted that the Christians should be slain. The leader of the other, that his word was pledged for their protection. A compromise was with difficulty made. Half the church was assigned to the Christians, half of it to Mohammedans. For some years the building was divided by an invisible line which Christians might not pass, though the space it bounded was consecrated to the worship of Christ.

This siege of Damascus was distinguished by the prowess of the Christian hero, Thomas. With incomparable bravery and skill he defended the principal gate until wounded by the wife of a Saracen he had slain, who indued her husband's armor, and, like a Joan of Arc, with her own courage reanimated her faltering countrymen.

The story of the Christian lovers, Jonas and Eudoxia, forms the theme of a tragedy by Mr. Hughes, which achieved great popularity in London during the last century.

While the lovers were attempting to escape together from the city, Jonas was captured by the Saracens. He renounced his faith, gained influence among his captors, and when by their assistance he had been reunited to Eudoxia, she stabbed herself to the heart as he clasped her in his arms.

It was Walid, the sixth caliph of the Omeiyades, says Porter, who compelled the Christians to surrender their part of the cathedral of St. John, and transformed it into the celebrated mosque. The vast wealth accumulated by plunder was used to rear a structure of surpassing splendor. Twelve hundred Greeks were employed upon the work. Columns of polished porphyry and granite were brought from Alexandria. The niches for prayer were framed in diamonds and other gems set in garlands of wrought gold. From the roof of carved wood, inlaid with precious metals, hung six hundred lamps, each of pure gold. Though plundered many times, the great mosque is still perhaps the noblest edifice in eastern Asia.

The most precious memory suggested by Damascus, we have not yet recalled. A young man of noble and sensitive spirit was fighting Christianity, because he verily thought he ought so to do. A few days before he visited the city, he had watched the death of Stephen, the first and noblest of Christian martyrs, the man of all men known to history most like himself. He was hastening to Damascus to kill others like Stephen. It cannot be but doubts had arisen in his mind. Could lies enable men to die as Stephen died? To men like Paul doubt is torment. "Suddenly there shone about him a light above the sun." Not many months before the man whose memory Paul hated had recognized doubt as the heaviest trouble good men have to bear. Referring to doubting John the Baptist, he had said, "Come unto me *all* ye that labor and are heavy laden, and I will give you rest! Take my yoke upon you and learn of me, for my yoke is easy!"

In the dazzling light Paul heard the same voice, using the same figure of an ox which will not accept its master's yoke but pushes back against the iron pointed goad, and saying to him, "It is hard for thee to kick against the pricks!" It seems to us that the Lord had been long watching Paul, pitying the struggles caused by a mistaken creed, and at last repeated to him, in slightly different language, the words spoken once before to help another doubter struggling in similar bewilderment. For these words, "It is hard for thee to kick against the pricks!" were only another way of saying, "*Take* my yoke and I will give thee rest!"

That Paul so understood them his future conduct proves. It seems appropriate that the great Apostle, who had been made a terror to others and a torment to himself by a false and fiendish creed, should find the peace that passeth understanding in that bright spot, which lies in the earth's dark shadow like a Christian's hope in the gloom of earthly desolations, the humble, homelike city of Damascus.

VIII.

TYRE, THE CITY OF MERCHANTS.

On the east shore of the Mediterranean, between the Gulf of Issus and Egypt, an extremely narrow belt of level land separates the sea from the mountains of Lebanon. A few miles south of Tyre the mountains reach the sea in an abrupt cliff called the " Tyrian Ladder," along which a road was carried in a gallery overhanging the water. South of the Tyrian Ladder, and interrupted only by the promontory of Carmel, the level widens into the maritime plain once inhabited by the Philistines, and named after them Philistia, or Palestine. North of the Tyrian Ladder the margin was called " Canaan," or " The Lowland."

Before historic times Canaan was occupied by a race of men named, probably from their swart complexions, Phœnicians or Red-Men. Their territory extended north a hundred and twenty miles, its breadth at no point exceeding twenty miles, often narrowed to one, and sometimes vanished between the mountains and the sea. It was fertilized by frequent streams descending from the mountains, and the mountains themselves supplied the best ship-timber known to the ancient world.

Before the age of Moses a score of little cities dotted this narrow territory. Excepting Tyre and Sidon they were, like the cities of Greece in later times, independent of each other; but, better tempered than Greek cities, they almost never quarreled. Incomparably the most important of them all was the one farthest south, called from its location "Tzur," or "The Rock." For this reason we take it as representative of the Phœnician race. Professor Rawlinson says that the Greeks, unable to pronounce the word correctly, and therefore softening it into Syr, called the region about Tyre Syria, and that the latter term, on account of its accidental resemblance in sound to Assur, was afterward applied to the far larger territory for which it stands. No other city, excepting only Jerusalem and Athens, has exerted an influence so immensely disproportionate to its size, and the genius of the three most important cities of the ancient world may be indicated by saying that Tyre cared for the bodies, Athens the minds, and Jerusalem the souls of men.

A strip of land twenty-eight miles long, never more than six miles broad, included both Tyre and Sidon, which were twenty miles apart, and embraced all of Phœnicia we need here to mention. Tyre alone was Phœnicia more truly than Athens was Greece. Whether Tyre or Sidon was the elder is uncertain, but before authentic history begins Tyre had taken the precedence, and both cities appear to have acknowledged the same king, who dwelt at Tyre, but is often called "King of the Sidonians."

Half a mile from the mainland a rock stood in the sea, exposing a rounded surface of something more than eighty acres. A short distance south of it arose a smaller rock showing an area above the water of between four and five acres. Both were fringed with reefs, and viewed together they resembled a shoe with an enormous instep and no heel, the toe turned north, and the sole pressing west toward the offing. In the day of Solomon, and how much earlier is not known, it is probable that a magnificent temple to the sun stood upon the larger rock.

The deity was worshiped under the name of Melkarth, or "King of the City," and was recognized by the Greeks as the Tyrian Hercules. Enormous shafts of red granite which probably adorned this temple have been found in the adjacent sea, deep buried beneath silt, and there is good reason to suppose that the edifice stood upon the highest part of the rock, so placed that the crest of Mount Hermon, the chief centre of Syrian sun worship, was conspicuous from its eastern court. A second temple, to the consort of the sun, seems to have stood upon the smaller rock. The identifications of these sites are purely conjectural, but they seem extremely probable.

Hiram appears to have been an enthusiast in building temples, and the artist and workmen sent by him to aid in erecting the celebrated structure at Jerusalem probably acquired their experience and skill in constructing sacred buildings for him upon the mainland near Tyre. We are told that Hiram sent to Solomon not only timber but carpenters to hew it. He had furnished Solomon's father with the masons who "built David an house," and it is not unreasonably inferred that he sent masons to help prepare the stones for the temple. The inference has been strengthened by excavations at Jerusalem. By means of shafts sunk eighty feet below the present surface of the ground, Captain Warren examined the foundation stones laid by Solomon, some of which are twenty and twenty-six feet in length. The calcium light revealed upon them Phœnician numerals, letters, and other signs in red paint, which are supposed to be quarry marks made by Hiram's masons.

At an early date some one — that it was Hiram himself is rendered probable by comparing the descriptions of Lieutenant Conder with a passage in Josephus — filled the channel between the two rocks on which his city stood. By the same means he joined the central mass and the surrounding reefs. Along the west side of the island, inlets, landing places, dry docks, very small in modern eyes, but large enough to accommodate the vessels used in Hiram's day, were cut in the solid rock. These cuttings are described by Lieutenant, now Captain, Conder, of the English navy. In the northeast of the island, facing the mainland, a harbor with a water area of twenty acres was called "The Port of Sidon," and a second, half that size, in the southeast, was named "The Egyptian Port."

The entire land area was less than a hundred and fifty acres. The enormous height of the houses enabled the city to accommodate between 30,000 and 40,000 inhabitants, and a very considerable population dwelt upon the adjacent mainland in times of peace. How or when we know not, the city girt itself with massive walls, the east line of which confronted Alexander the Great with an elevation of a hundred and fifty feet. The buildings and the walls have vanished. Their fragments shallow the surrounding waters. But excepting one change made by Alexander, the site probably remains nearly as it was left by King Hiram.

Tyre may rank third among cities in weight of influence upon the human race. For she taught mankind effectually three facts which had to be in some way discovered, and in some degree believed, before the world could be prepared by Athens for the teachings of Jerusalem. The facts were these: That the sea was not designed to sever but to unite the nations. That peace is more profitable than war. That it is more blessed to give than to receive.

Before Tyre launched her ships, the ocean was simply a terror to men. It formed the impassable barrier of their migrations. It was the mysterious mother of storms. The most dreaded monsters of their mythologies inhabited the sea. Man's safety was felt to lie in keeping well away from them on land. The Tyrians broke the spell. They sailed forth despite the monsters. They sailed by the north star, which for that reason the Greeks called the Phœnician star. Because it guided them safely, the Tyrians worshiped it together with the moon under the name of Astarte. Wise Solomon offered to build ships on the Red Sea, if Hiram would man them, and Tyrian sailors divided the wealth of the Indies between Tyre and Jerusalem. In a later age Jehoshaphat attempted to navigate the same waters without the Tyrian sailors, and his vessels were splintered upon the rocks of Ezion Geber before they had fairly got to sea. While the Greeks still regarded Theseus for sailing beyond the Hellespont as we regard Columbus, Tyrian sailors had crossed the Mediterranean. They planted colonies in Utica, Carthage, and Cadiz; passed the pillars of Hercules, and covered their little rock with gold from Spain, tin from Cornwall, and amber from the Baltic. Two thousand years before Vasco di Gama astounded Europe by doubling the Cape of Good Hope, Tyrians had circumnavigated Africa, and provoked the incredulity of Herodotus by telling of regions where the sun always cast the shadows south. Cadem in Semitic tongues means east, Europe in the same means west, and the fables of Cadmus bringing letters into Greece and Europa swimming forth from Tyre were Greek ways of keeping in mind that Europe owed to Tyre both her education and her enterprise. The facts by no means rest upon a basis of mythology. Wherever Phœnicians learned them, — some say from Egypt, some say from Chaldæa, and the latter seem correct, — it is certain that Tyre taught Greece her letters, and the enormous wealth which Tyre had found in Spain, the ancient Peru, eventually excited the cupidity of Greece and sent her young men also sailing after golden fleeces.

There is no other discipline which so rapidly develops in men hardihood, courage, and mental alertness as the discipline of contending with waves and winds upon the ocean. Proof of that statement abounds in the histories of the Saxons, the Danes, the Hollanders, and in the histories of Maine and Massachusetts. No ancient people approached the Phœnicians in seamanship, and no people, ancient or modern, have equaled them in the energy and endurance by which their skill in seamanship was gained. Therefore, the Tyrians became the bravest of ancient peoples, and the most fertile in resource.

Because they were so brave they were able to teach the profitableness of peace. They attacked no one. They made friends with all. What they desired they sought to obtain by fair exchange, and so taught mankind the meaning of the word "Com-merce," or "Mutual-reward," and were the first to prove by their example that commerce was more remunerative than pillage.

The Phœnicians had somewhere learned that it is more blessed to give than to receive. They were the first peaceful colonizers. Other nations sought increase of power and population by conquest only. They knew how to take whole peoples captive, plant them in subject cities, or use them as slaves. Tyre inverted that policy. She had caught some whisper of the voice which bids men found a kingdom by forsaking father and mother, if need be, and giving themselves. Few as they were in numbers the Tyrians very early began sending forth men and women to found other cities in distant places for the common benefit, not only of those at home, but of those among whom they went. So arose Utica, or Old Town, and near it Carthage, or New Town, and Cadiz in Spain.

Other sunny memories might be added from the history of ancient Tyre. The generous manhood of Tyrian sailors is vividly portrayed in the noble poem of Jonah. Zeno, who came near discovering that all men under heaven are of one blood, and should therefore count each other brothers, was the son of a Tyrian merchant, and is thought by Mr. Merivale to have been born at Tyre.

But through her religion Tyre exercised a baleful influence upon the ancient world. From her both Syria and Greece received the worst of their abominations. From her, by help of Moab, Israel learned to make "her children pass through fire unto Moloch."

There was fast friendship between King David and King Hiram. They spoke slightly different dialects of the same language, and were joined by many ties of mutual advantage. This Tyrian friendship continued beyond the age of Solomon, and its fatal fascination caused the ruin of Israel when the fierce but fascinating Jezebel, the only person Elijah ever feared, came from Tyre to bewitch Ahab, fight the great reformer, and receive at last, by a horrible death, her merited reward. There was never open war between Israel and Tyre, but the friendship between them had cooled in the age of the prophet Joel, who denounced Tyrian merchants for selling Hebrew slaves to foreigners. In view of these denunciations it is interesting to read on the clay tablet found at Nineveh the contract of a Tyrian merchant with an Assyrian lady for the sale of two Hebrew slaves.

The oldest historic mention of Tyre occurs in a papyrus manuscript now in the British Museum. It is one of the oldest manuscripts in the world. It was written before the age of Joshua, and appears to be the letter of an official sent by Pharaoh to inspect the military posts in Syria, to a friend in Egypt. The writer laments the badness of the roads, tells how his chariot broke down, and compelled him to spend twenty-four hours in a stupid village while the blacksmith made repairs; relates how his baggage was stolen by a thief while he slept, and his heart by a lovely lady when he awoke; and adds that he had visited Sidon, Sarepta, and "Tyre on the sea, to which water is carried in barks, and which is richer in fishes than in sands."

The last allusion to Tyre I shall quote was written by Renan, some twenty years ago. "Phœnicia is the only country in the world in which the industrial arts have left magnificent remains. A wine press there resembles a triumphal arch. Industrial appliances with us so fragile are there colossal. The Phœnicians built presses and fish ponds for eternity. In the neighborhood of Tyre, these primitive remains are found upon almost every height."

We have noticed the kind of discipline by which the Tyrians were trained. Though loath to make war they were prompt to repel invasion. Three of the many recorded sieges of their city equal in heroism of resistance the defense of Saragossa.

Five years Tyre held out against the whole power of Assyria, under Shalmaneser. When

Nebuchadnezzar, one of the ablest, perhaps the ablest monarch before Cæsar, had conquered Egypt and the Orient, Tyre was the only city which successfully defied him. For thirteen years he besieged it, and there is no proof that the long siege was successful, though the rest of Phœnicia yielded to him.

When the battle of Issus had crushed the power of Persia, other cities hastened to send Alexander tokens of surrender. But Tyre, true to her traditions, defied him. He began a siege which lasted seven months. He was forced to call every ship he could command to aid in the blockade, while he pressed the attack by building that stupendous mole which still joins the island to the mainland, and has changed the outline of the place from a shoe into a boot. Inch by inch the Tyrians fought him. They invented engines of defense formidable as his engines of assault. When at last the conqueror entered the city, he razed the walls, left it a desert, and carried 30,000 captives into slavery. Superstition or policy moved him to treat with reverence the temple of Melkarth, or Hercules, and liberate those defenders who had sought refuge within its walls.

In the twelfth century Tyre was captured

by the crusaders. After a brief period of triumph the cross had begun to retreat before the crescent, when the Venetians, convinced that it would benefit their commerce to do so, were persuaded to take arms against the Saracens. They sent a powerful fleet to Palestine, which on the way thither attacked and put to flight the fleet of their Christian brethren of Genoa. The Council of Jerusalem could not determine whether to attack Askelon or Tyre. They wrote the names of the two cities upon separate parchments, and laid them upon the altar in the Church of the Holy Sepulchre. An orphan child, doubtless with appropriate ceremonies, was led between lines of kneeling warriors, to the altar, and bidden to take one of the parchments. He took that which bore the name of Tyre. By this fierce perversion of Isaiah's prophecy, "a little child shall lead them," the crusaders were convinced that God directed them to Tyre. The whole Venetian navy blockaded the little city on the west, — remember how small it was, less than a hundred and fifty acres, — while the entire crusading army assaulted from the east. Month after month the brave defenders held out, returning blow for blow. The land forces at last lost heart. They refused to continue the attack. The Venetians who, like the ancient Tyrians, had gathered their courage from the sea, landed, entered the camp of their allies each carrying an oar upon his shoulder, and declared they would fight their way across the mole with oars, as the Franks could not take it with their spears. Shamed by the taunt, the army renewed the attack, and Tyre was taken.

There seems to have been a contagion of courage in the stones of Tyre. In 1188, when Saladin had conquered Jerusalem, Tyre, now in Christian hands, checked his victorious career as she had checked of old the careers of Nebuchadnezzar and of Alexander. The French soldier, Conrad of Montferrat, commanded the defense. His aged father had been taken prisoner in the battle of Tiberias. Saladin summoned the city to surrender. Conrad refused. The citizens resolved man by man to perish rather than open their gates to the enemy. Saladin threatened to advance with Conrad's father bound in front of his army, a target for missiles shot from either side. " I will shoot the first arrow, and when my father falls thank God I am the son of a Christian martyr!" was Conrad's reply.

Saladin could not fulfill his threat. Brave men do not easily succeed when they try to act as dastards. But the Saracens attacked, they fought bravely, wisely, and long, but they could not take the city.

In 1291 Tyre died. We say a man dies when his spirit leaves his body. Therefore we say Tyre died. The same day upon which Acre fell the Tyrians deserted their city. Without protest, without debate, without a blow in her defense, those who should have been her protectors fled in their vessels. They stole away by night and left the gates, which Nebuchadnezzar and Saladin had vainly tried to force, open to the enemy. The craven citizens hoped their cowardice would save them, and refused to countenance resistance. The Saracens entered unopposed. A massacre ensued. "The Musselmans," says Michaud, "seemed to wish to destroy the very earth on which the Christians trod; their houses, their temples, the monuments of their piety, their valor, and their industry, everything was condemned to perish with them by the sword or by fire."

From this destruction Tyre never rose again, but she still lingered on, a body without a soul, until captured by the Turks in

1516, and made by them the desolation she appears to-day.

Enough has perhaps been said to suggest the question: "How could Tyre be so great without being greater? Why did she vanish so utterly from history? Why did she leave no monuments? Why has she who gave letters to Greece left no literature beyond a few paltry inscriptions like those exhumed by Di Cesnola in Cyprus, no art remains beyond the poor bronzes whose shattered fragments, pieced together by M. Clermont Ganneau, tell us they once formed a vase offered by a King Hiram to God Melkarth?"

The answer is at hand. Americans would do well to ponder it. Tyre thought she worshiped Melkarth. She did worship Mammon. The absorbing object of her enterprise was wealth. To win riches, she exercised a wisdom and an energy never equaled by the children of light in their quest of better things. "Seek ye first the kingdom of God and his righteousness, and other good things shall be added unto you," is the law of life omnipotent upon this planet. To invert that law, to seek first other good things in hope that righteousness will at last be added, is to obey the law of death equally omnipotent. That Tyre did, and therefore Tyre perished, and perished utterly.

IX.

ATHENS, THE CITY OF CULTURE.

ATHENS attained to the height of her splendor about 444 B. C. The period of her most important service to the world began a century later. At the first date she was a dandelion in blossom, the loveliest of flowers. At the latter she was the same dandelion when the winds begin to drive its ripe seeds to the work for which wings are given them.

The battle of Issus, 333 B. C., marks the most important date in Grecian annals, if we measure history, as we pretend to do, from the year of our Lord, and recognize the chief significance of events in the relations they bear to the Saviour of the world. For Athens prepared the electric wires by which the word of God was carried from Jerusalem to the ends of the earth, and at Issus Alexander began their ultimate adjustment.

A unique civic atmosphere fitted Athens for her mission.

Imagine that no Bibles, or almost none, exist in the city where you live, while yet, in some way, all your fellow citizens have become more familiar with the contents of the Bible than any one of them actually is. The leaves of the book, we will suppose, were torn apart years ago, and scattered through the streets, where every verse turned into a picture, and every parable and prophecy into a marble group. Wealth we will suppose has never been fashionable among your people. Riches can win no prestige except by being used for the public benefit. No one cares to live in a finer house, or to dress more expensively than his neighbors, for to do so provokes contempt or ridicule, and gets one called a barbarian. Public revenues and private fortunes have been generally devoted to making the city a visible reproduction of the Bible. The store fronts are frescoed with illustrations of Solomon's proverbs. The main street is named " St. John's," and before each house upon it stands a marble bust of the disciple whom Jesus loved. The central avenue is appropriately called " Cross Street," from the endless variety of crosses, one of which appears in metal or in marble before every door that opens into it. Other avenues are called after different saints, and instead of their names written at the corners, stand their busts or statues, which one must be able to recognize, or he cannot find his way. There is no spot in the city where one can open his eyes without beholding a sculpture or a fresco that illustrates some Scriptural scene or doctrine. There is no spot from which a church adorned with statues of Scriptural characters is not conspicuous. Instead of capitol or court house, a church occupies the most conspicuous location in the city, and beside it, towering above its spire, a colossal image of Jesus upon the cross marks the spot where all the citizens believe their Lord was crucified.

The theatres are open to the sky. Every one frequents them. The front seats are reserved for ministers and magistrates. Each performance is opened with prayer, and the serious plays written by men who have had few peers and no superiors are based upon the Bible.

The innumerable statues which adorn the churches, theatres, and streets, the buildings of which the outer walls are not painted in plain colors but frescoed with Scripture scenes by artists such as Polygnotus and Apelles, even the busts which serve for signs at the street corners, have been executed by men whose works will remain for two thousand years the unapproachable standards of loveliness for the human race. Indeed the ablest art critic of our century implies that a statue by Michael Angelo might rank beside one of Phidias as a stone mason's cutting beside the Theseus of Canova. Add to all this that on the Public Park one or more of half a dozen men whose equals in mental ability the world has scarcely produced outside of Israel wait every day to converse upon the most important themes of morals and religion with all who care to hear them, and that other men do throng to profit by their wisdom.

If the reader will imagine all this, he will have a more adequate conception of Athens in her prime than details of archæology can give him. For Homer and Hesiod were the Greek Bible. The Athenians believed their Bible. Convinced that their goddess had founded their city and still guided its affairs, their current history was to them a constantly augmenting New Testament. Poets, artists, and teachers spent their lives illustrating and enforcing the contents of this Bible. Their amusements were a part of the religion it taught, and the wealth of the city was lavished in making her citizens as Paul found them, exceedingly religious. Excepting that religion of which the law was given by Moses, while the grace and truth of its law appeared in Jesus Christ, no religion among mankind has been developed by so much mental ability, popularized by so much genius, accepted and practiced with so great fidelity, as that of Athens; and none has ended in a more hopeless anarchy of Atheism and despair.

Nowhere else has the human mind attained such strength, nowhere else has culture been so general and so diffused, as in Attica the fifth century before Christ. "A population of 90,000," says Francis Galton, in substance, "produced in a hundred years two men, Socrates and Phidias, by whose side we have none to place, because the whole population of Europe in 2,000 years has not produced their equals. In the same period the same population of 90,000 gave birth to fourteen men whose intellectual equals have been produced four or five times by the Anglo-Saxon race in the entire period of its history." "It follows," says the same authority, " that the average ability of the Athenian race was on the lowest possible estimate very nearly two grades higher than our own (the English) ; that is about as much as our race is above the African negro."

Without pressing this conclusion, though it comes from high authority and is confirmed by strong and varied proofs, a glance at Athenian civilization, with its growing and ripened profligacies, its deliberate cruelties, its jealousies of every neighbor, and the frantic passions which rent its own bosom and finally destroyed its life, may suffice to teach us that no amount of popular education or mental ability without Him who was named Jesus can save a people from their sins.

Let us visit Athens some 444 years before the Saviour's birth. We will enter through the northwest or "Double Gate," the only one as yet identified with certainty. Inside the walls we pass eastward between two colonnades of white marble called porches. They are roofed. On the sides fronting the street the spaces between the columns are open. On the inner sides the columns are united by surfaces of white marble, which they frame as pictures. The structure upon the left hand is dedicated to the God of Liberty. It is filled with sculptures and its inner wall and ceiling are frescoed with a series of scenes illustrating the history of Athens from the earliest times. The structure beyond it, frescoed by Polygnotus with scenes from the battle of Marathon, is called the Painted Porch or Stoa. Passing beyond these porches, and bending southeastward, we cross Hermes Street. We cannot pause to scrutinize the lovely busts of Hermes which stand in front of every house, but hastening forward descend into a valley not deep, but shaped as if a spoon half a mile in length with a handle extremely short and a bowl extremely shallow had left its impress upon the ground. At the centre of the bowl, which is an accurate ellipse, stands an altar to the twelve great gods. Here starts and terminates every road connecting Athens with the rest of the world. The major axis of the ellipse, along which we have come, is less than the third of a mile in length, and the ellipse itself, inclosed by buildings and colonnades, contains statues of every Olympic deity and of the most illustrious Athenians. The statues of Harmodius and Aristogeiton occupy the position of honor at the southeast entrance, near the foot of the Acropolis. This ellipse is the place of business and industrial activity. It is divided into sections occupied by different trades, and each section is marked by the statue of its patron deity. It is also the parlor of the city, the place for conversation. Here statesmen, generals, poets, philosophers, merchants, and artisans meet as social equals. There has never been in any other time or place such complete fraternity of classes as prevailed among the citizens of ancient Athens. The equality we feign in Christian churches existed there. The ellipse we have tried to describe was called the Agora, and is in the New Testament inadequately rendered "Market Place."

Before that cobbler's bench a little crowd has gathered. They are listening to Socrates. He has asked the cobbler some question about leather, and the answer has led on to one of those conversations which, reproduced by Plato, will be cherished by the world among its most precious intellectual treasures.

While Socrates is talking, a trumpet has

sounded. In obedience to the signal, other parts of the Agora have been deserted. But it is not strange that those near Socrates have failed to hear the summons. Neither have they noticed men stretching between them ropes stained with vermilion powder, and racing across the Agora as if to sweep it clear. All who notice fly before the runners, for the rope marks with a smirch of red each man it touches, and citizens so marked will be recognized as late or absent from the meeting of the legislature, and fined, for every citizen belongs to the general court, and is obliged to attend its sessions. The trumpet has called them together, and those who are not present at the opening prayers will have to pay the fine. The citizens thus summoned by the trumpet were named, to distinguish them from the slaves, " the called ones " or the " ecclesia." This is the name so dear to Paul, the " ecclesia " or " Church," which signified men called by Jesus Christ to be kings and priests, as the citizens of Athens were called to their place of legislation.

We look up to see the trumpeter. We are facing southeast, and standing in the centre of the Agora. On our left hand, conspicuous above all intervening buildings, just outside the limits of the Agora, rises the hill named Areopagus. The trumpeter is not there. On our right, a little farther off, is a larger hill called "Museum" because a mythical prophet named Museus is supposed to have been buried upon it. The trumpeter is not there. Directly before us, bounding the Agora southeastward, is a still higher elevation, the Acropolis or Citadel. The trumpeter is not there. We would have been wiser to follow Socrates. Directly behind us, whither he has gone, at the western end of the Agora, stands a hill called Pnyx, or the "Place of Assemblies," from a root suggesting fists, because the fist is made by bringing the fingers together. Cut in the solid rock of this hill is a theatre open to the sky, and large enough to seat six thousand citizens, with two square yards of space for each. The speaker's stand, a portion of the native rock left in place, is called "the Step" or "Bema." It belongs alike to all, and each speaker to ascend it must step forth from the other citizens as from among his equals. Beside this Bema stands the trumpeter. Socrates sits near him, and Pericles is rising to address the Assembly. In a later generation, Demosthenes and Eschines will follow him.

Four centuries and more after Pericles, Paul was standing possibly upon the spot where we first saw Socrates — for it has not been proved that a new Agora had supplanted the old. Certainly Paul was talking, as Socrates had talked, with the man he had found nearest at hand, when the listeners who had gathered around him invited the Apostle to prolong his discourse, and conducted him for that purpose to the more secluded Areopagus. Thither let us follow. Steep steps cut in the face of the rock lead upward to it. Upon the rounded summit of the hill are the stone seats of the judges who try capital cases and of the officials who manage the religious affairs of the city. Before these are two large stones — probably surmounted by short metal pillars. On one is inscribed "Implacable," on the other, "Crime." Upon these stones accuser and accused must stand facing each other, and plead their own causes before the most august tribunal of Athens. In close proximity below it is the temple of Conscience, whose stings the Greeks with fine intuition named at once "The Tormentors" and "The Wellwishers," or Erinnys and Eumenides.

Descending once more into the Agora, we move southeast along its major axis toward the Acropolis. Behind us rises the Pnyx hill, where we left Socrates; on our left, the Areopagus, where we leave Paul; on our right, the Museum; before us, the Acropolis. The ascent to it, three hundred feet, slopes steeply upward from the Agora for a few paces, then rises abruptly. By steps hewn in the rock we approach the summit. The stairway terminates in the most splendid gateway ever seen on earth. Through a vestibule of sculptured white marble glowing with color, on the right hand a marble wing balancing the most superb gallery of pictures in Athens, on the left, we pass through either of five entrances which open with folding doors of massive bronze upon the summit of the Acropolis. It is a leveled rock, the highest in the city, a thousand feet from east to west, five hundred north to south, descending sheer on every side except the west, and accessible only by the stairway we have surmounted. Near the south verge, facing east, upon the crest of the city, stands the Parthenon, not, as we imagine it, a cold white miracle of beauty, but glowing with gold and color. Opposite, upon the north verge, stands a smaller temple consecrated to the same goddess, the Erectheum, the supreme model of Ionic as is the Parthenon of Doric grace.

The space between these temples and the entire surface of the Acropolis is covered with a forest of statues. In the centre of this forest, midway between her two temples, facing west and raised upon a lofty pedestal, stands the Colossus of Athena. Cast by Phidias from the spoils of Marathon; seventy feet in height, with spear and shield and helmet, it towers above every other structure in Athens, the first object seen by the sailors as they round the cape of Sunium.

We will view the city through the eyes of the statue. Southwestward two parallel lines of military defense called the "Long walls" protect the road to Piræus harbor. Conspicuous beyond them rises the lofty steep of Ægaleos, whence Xerxes watched the sea fight which drove him back to Susa, to be tricked by Haman and saved by Queen Esther.

"A king sat on the rocky brow
That looks o'er sea-born Salamis,
And ships by thousands lay below,
And men in nations; all were his.
He counted them at break of day,
And at sunset where were they?"

Sweeping around the plain west, north, east, the mountains ascend in graceful slopes, at points advancing to within a mile of the walls. Two miles away, upon the northwest, winds the Cephissus; half a mile to the south, the Ilissus. The city is girt with cemeteries so exquisitely laid out with flowers, statues, and porches as to be the favorite resorts of leisure. The loveliest lies northwest. There are the graves of the most illustrious patriots. There among the flowers and the marbles, Lysias pronounced the Funeral Oration. In this vicinity, on the banks of the Cephissus, but precisely where is not yet known, in a suburb called The Academy, was the garden in which Plato taught.

Within the walls, and near the gate by which we entered, the Painted Porch or Stoa is full in view. The man who will in a hundred years be seen walking to and fro behind its columns, surrounded by a throng of youths, and pausing at times to emphasize his words by pointing to the pictures of Marathon upon the inner wall, is the son of a Tyrian merchant. He was bringing a cargo of merchandise from Cyprus, was wrecked near Sunium, and has since spent his time in teaching the young men of

Athens truths which, three hundred years later, will form during two centuries the religion of the wisest and best of both Greece and Rome. His name is Zeno, and his disciples are called, from their place of meeting, Stoics or "Porch men," as the disciples of Plato are called men of the Academy.

Southward, on the banks of the Ilissus, appears a temple to Apollo, the "Wolf-slayer," or "Lyceus." In the adjacent grove, called from its nearness to the temple, "The Lyceum," Aristotle will teach. If one chose to give loose rein to fancy, he might discern in the name a prediction of the day when the renewed study of Aristotle will begin to destroy in mediæval Europe the superstitions which almost devoured Christendom. Bible exegetes have often belittled the Scriptures they meant to exalt by attempts to prove their inspiration from coincidences even more fantastic.

We know not where, but at some point within the city walls, and, though the evidence is purely conjectural, quite probably upon Museum Hill, was another famous garden. It was occupied by a society of men and women unlike any seen before it, and not unlike that Brook Farm community to which Margaret Fuller, Emerson, and Hawthorne have given a wide celebrity. The master and teacher was Epicurus, a noble and self-denying man, whose doctrines, abused and quite inverted by his later followers, became at last a philosophy of formulated vice.

It is evident from what has preceded, that Athens was distinctively a city of talkers; of talkers in that noblest sense of the term which underlies its meaning, when Christ is named the "Word of God." The Agora was a parlor or place of conversation. The city was filled with porches, and surrounded with gardens, where men resorted to talk. Every citizen was a member of the legislature, and there was prompted by ambition to learn the art of effective speech. Before the court of Areopagus, plaintiff and defendant must each plead his own cause. The banquets of Aspasia, a magnificent and greatly slandered woman, were types of many others where food and wine were forgotten in the main purpose of the meeting, which was conversation. The most influential Athenians were those who could talk most ably.

Three results were inevitable from such a

soil and climate. A language was developed which has never been equaled in power, range, and accuracy of expression, and in melody of sound. The Greek tongue excels all other tongues, as Greek art transcends all other art. A sentiment was generated and diffused which counted mental more precious than material riches, and realized that a man's life consists not in the abundance of the things he possesses, but in that which he is. Because they were mentally the ablest, the most cultivated, and in all powers of expression, whether music, art, or speech, immeasurably the most gifted of mankind, the Greeks naturally became the teachers of the race, so that eventually every revelation made in Greek came with wings. The religion of Israel, which had limped in Hebrew, flew when it was translated into Greek. The same hand which in Palestine prepared the bread of life, in Greece constructed the vehicle for its distribution. In the age of Xerxes, Greek influence had begun to pervade the East. The campaigns of Alexander made that influence predominant. When Aristotle had taught the great Macedonian all he could of Athenian culture, the eastern campaign began. In ten years, by a career of conquest as yet unparalleled, Alexander overran western Asia and a great part of India. Hundreds of Greek cities sprang up in all parts of these vast dominions. Greek thought, Greek customs, and especially the Greek language, became domesticated from the Nile to the Euphrates. At Alexander's death the world split into three empires, ruled by three of his generals. But the brain and heart of Greece was not Macedon, but still Athens. At Alexandria Ptolemy Soter had the Hebrew Scriptures translated into Greek, and the commerce of the world was put into the hands of Greeks. These influences worked subtly but steadily, until the time of Christ. At no other period of the world's history has so weighty a proportion of the human race been acquainted with a single language as was familiar with Greek when Paul began to preach. It was the language of commerce, of literature, of fashion, of everything but war. In this language the Apostles delivered their message. In it the New Testament was written, and into it the Old Testament had already been translated.

Thus Athens laid the wires over which the word of God was flashed to the ends of the earth. Thus Athens did for men's minds what Tyre did for their bodies. Without the Greek language prepared at Athens by centuries of intellectual activity, the New Testament could not have been written, for no other tongue possessed resources adequate to the requirements of either John or Paul. Without the Greek language, diffused from Macedon and Alexandria, Christianity could not, for centuries, at least, have been "preached to all nations." Without those cravings excited by Grecian thought, and tantalized by Greek philosophies which could not satisfy them, men would not have been ready to receive the gospel. The thirsts generated by the Ilissus, which to-day is dry, led them to Him who alone could give the living waters which flow forever.

Athens, the palace of beauty, the citadel of mind, the throne of culture, her beauty dissolved, her citadel in ruins, her culture ending in a horror of great darkness — an anarchy of epicurean sensuality or stoical despair — Athens totally unable to discover or invent a religion adequate to human needs, is the most convincing witness to man's need of Him who came down from heaven to give life unto the world.

X.

ROME, THE CITY OF THE LAW-GIVERS.

SOMEWHERE in the suburbs of Jerusalem, the exact locality is doubtful, was a spot, probably a little hill, which was called in the Hebrew tongue, Golgotha, in Latin, Calvary, in English, "The place of a skull." Here, where some have supposed the configuration of the ground suggested a skull, and others that a burial-place reminded of death, a throne was placed and laws promulgated. The throne was a cross, and the laws were the Sermon on the Mount.

On the left bank of the Tiber, fourteen miles above its mouth, was a little hill called the place of the Head, in Latin the Capitol. A myth derived its name from the discovery upon it of a human head, by men digging for the foundations of a temple, but the name was probably given to mark the spot as the seat of authority and the source of national life. Here a sceptre was lifted and laws promulgated. The sceptre was a sword, and the laws the wisest and the best which have ever depended upon the sword for their enforcement.

Upon the hill of death at Jerusalem the cross and the sword fought their first battle, and there the sword appeared to be the stronger. Three centuries later they met again at the place of life in Rome, in a crisis which proved that the cross had been the stronger. The most important story Rome can tell is the conquest of the Capitol by Calvary.

A little southeast of the Capitoline was a second hill, called for unknown reasons the Palatine. Upon this Romulus was said to have been suckled, and his straw-thatched hut was reverently exhibited in the days of Julius Cæsar. The valley between these hills was originally a marsh. During the dry season it formed a battle-ground for the two hostile tribes which occupied the adjacent eminences, but when the Sabines on the Capitoline, and the Latins on the Palatine had been united under a single government, the marsh, drained by an enormous sewer, became the heart of Rome, and eventually of the empire.

We will visit it upon the 15th day of

March, 44 B. C., and take our stand upon a low platform, at the base of the Capitoline hill, facing southeast, toward the Palatine. Before us lies an open space paved with blocks of travertine. It is three hundred and seventy-five feet long, and narrows regularly, as it leaves us, from a breadth of one hundred and fifty to one of one hundred and ten feet. It is inclosed by buildings which, extending in all directions, form the wilderness of Rome. It is the "Great Forum." The platform beneath us, raised eleven feet above the general level, paved and faced with white marble, and fenced with a railing of gilded metal, is a rectangle seventy-eight feet broad, and projecting half that distance into the Forum. It is probably near this platform that Augustus will place a bronze column, will inscribe upon it, in gold letters, the name and distance of every important city on the roads leaving Rome, and call it the "Golden Milestone." From the opposite side of the platform the bronze beaks of ships, captured in battle, project over the pavement of the Forum. They are called Rostra. From them the platform is called the Rostra, and from its builder, the Julian Rostra.

On this day, March 15, 44 B. C., the corpse of Cæsar, "marred as you see by traitors," lay exposed upon this platform, while Mark Antony pronounced the speech commemorated by Shakespeare.

A careless eye reads in the bronze beaks that Rome is mistress of the sea; in the golden milestone that she rules the land; and sees in the body of Cæsar the man who gained her an almost universal sovereignty. The bronze beaks, the golden milestone, and the bleeding corpse combine to tell a more thoughtful observer that Cæsar was only the ablest of many journeymen executing the plans of a master builder they never knew, who was soon to reveal himself at Bethlehem.

I would have you observe from the Julian Rostra four objects, one on the right, one on the left, one in the centre, and one beyond the opposite extremity of the Great Forum. They stand for the laws, the wars, the amusements, and the religion of ancient Rome.

I. On the left of the Forum, distant from us half its length, a small square shrine of polished bronze gleams like gold. Through either of its four open doors is visible a rude two-faced image, with fingers twisted into the Latin numerals, representing three hundred and fifty-five, the number of days in the Latin year. It is the Etruscan Janus, god of time and war, after whom the first month in our year is named. By its side is an exquisite marble by a Greek artist, stolen from Athens, and feigned to represent the same divinity. The four bronze gates, always open in time of war, and closed but twice since Rome began to be, must soon be shut for the birth of the Prince of Peace.

At his birth Rome had attained a vast population which has been variously estimated by scholars. Her empire reached from the Thames to the Euphrates, and from Germany to the African desert and the Persian Gulf. It had been won by war. To establish their conquests, the Romans were accustomed to build a military road to the heart of every province the instant it had been subdued. No conquest was thought complete until this had been done. By relays of horses kept in fortified posts, couriers moved from the golden milestone to all important centres of the empire at the rate of a hundred miles a day. Ships plied constantly from the Tiber to all Mediterranean ports. At the birth of Christ, for the first time in history, communication between peoples speaking "every language under heaven" was frequent, safe, and rapid. In eastern Asia travel was easier and more secure than it is to-day. When the land had been threaded with roads, and the sea made a highway by men building better than they knew, the command was given, "Go, preach the gospel to all nations." It could be obeyed, because the men of war had prepared the way before the messengers of peace.

II. Opposite the temple of Janus, on the right of the Forum, stood the Basilica Julia, a court-house, begun by Julius Cæsar and completed by Augustus. Its plan was reproduced in the public buildings erected for Christian worship until very recent times. During the first two centuries of our era, Christians built no churches. They held their meetings in private houses. But when church building began, it largely copied the Roman court-house.

The basilica stood for Roman law. It was needful that the men sent forth to "disciple" all nations should be protected while they did their errand. For this purpose the nations must be controlled by laws protecting life and personal liberty. The Romans were the world's consummate law-givers. They represented authority. Their legislation forms the basis of most European codes except the English, and has been influential even there. Those who exercise authority are still called by Roman names: President, Emperor, Cæsar (modified into the German Kaiser and the Russian Czar), sovereign, or superior, Senator, Congressman, Legislator, Pope (which is Latin for father), Cardinal (which means "chief man"). These names are all inherited from Rome, and the most august ecclesiastical organization which has yet existed perpetuates in the name "Roman Catholic Church" the memory of the unequaled skill with which the Imperial City controlled all classes of men.

Roman laws were, in most respects, just and beneficent. Had they not been, no amount of force could have held the nations so long in subjection to them. Neither would the conscience of Christendom have retained them in its codes. Roman law saved Paul's life many times, and enabled him to fight the good fight and finish his course. Without it Christianity would have been murdered in its cradle. To citizens just and equable, to slaves it afforded no protection. For this reason, I think, Christ chose to die a slave's death. We read of Roman ladies torturing female slaves who had failed to satisfy their vanity at the toilet; of Roman masters feeding to their fishes the minced flesh of slaves who had provoked them. Doubtless such freaks of passion were exceptional, and indulged chiefly to terrorize a class grown formidable from its numbers and ability. But these and worse atrocities than these occurred unrebuked, and even Cicero and Seneca taught that it was a duty to regard slaves not as human beings, but as dogs and cattle. Soon after the death of Christ, a Christian sentiment began to appear, first in their treatment, and eventually in the laws which regulated their treatment. This sentiment marked the first step toward the conversion of the Roman Empire.

III. Near the centre of the Forum, between the temple of Janus and the Basilica Julia, appeared at times, long before Cæsar, a slight and temporary wooden structure, arranged for gladiatorial exhibitions. The Etruscans sacrificed slaves at the funerals of distinguished men. Human sacrifices are known to have been prohibited, and therefore were probably practiced at Rome as late as 87 B. C. Two hundred and sixty-four years before Christ the father of Decimus Brutus died. The son celebrated his funeral by arming slaves and bidding them slay each other. The spectacle won the favor of the populace. It was afterwards imitated in the Forum for the public entertainment. For these exhibitions temporary structures were erected. In the reign of Vespasian this seed had grown into the Colosseum. The genius of Roman manners was there revealed even more distinctively than in the great circus, which was larger, and seated more than 380,000 spectators.

A man's character is shown most correctly not in the things he does because he must, but in those he does because he likes to do them; not in his business, but in his amusements. It is so with a people. Therefore we will visit the Colosseum to study Rome.

The Colosseum was in plain view from the Great Forum southeastward along the Sacred Street. It occupied the site of an artificial lake which Nero had constructed for sea fights in the garden of his "Golden House." Every reader is familiar with its outlines.

The arena or floor was wood, and formed an ellipse with a major axis of 281, and a minor of 176 feet. Beneath the floor was a labyrinth of supporting arches, sinuous passage-ways, cages or cells for wild beasts, water conduits and drains, and marvelous machinery for the production of scenic effects. The arena was inclosed by a wall of white marble eleven feet high, surmounted by a fence of gilded metal bars. The top bars were cylinders which revolved at a touch, so that if a panther should leap the eighteen feet and clutch one of them it would turn and drop the beast back again inside the barrier. Immediately outside this barrier and rising above it ran a continuous marble platform profusely decorated with statues and broad enough for two ranges of movable seats, which were reserved for the emperor, the court, and the vestal virgins. The four entrances were at the extremities of the axes of the ellipse. The north entrance opened near the emperor's throne and was connected by a covered way with his palace upon the Esquiline.

Behind the marble platform, which was called the Podium, tiers of white marble, sloping upward and backward, afforded seats for 87,000 spectators, while wooden tiers ascending still higher accommodated half as many more. A line of decorated masts rimmed the arena. On spectacle days these were joined by festoons of flowers, and from their tops canopies of silk, stretched by ropes of variegated colors attached to the outer walls, screened the audience from the sun. The air was cooled by jets of perfumed water shot in vapors from hidden tubes. The seats of the wealthy were cushioned with silk and cloth of gold. Though the Colosseum had not yet been built, a scene such as appeared to the runner who glanced upward from the arena while 100,000 faces bending eagerly toward him were blended into misty outlines by the distance was in the mind of the inspired writer when, to make us realize the sympathy heavenly watchers feel for earthly toilers, he wrote, "Seeing we also are compassed about by so great a cloud of witnesses, let us lay aside every weight and the sin which doth so easily beset us, and let us run with patience the race that is set before us."

Each seat in the vast amphitheatre was numbered, and the ivory check for it must be held by its occupant. One such check dug up in the Campagna, sixty miles from Rome, is marked "Section 6. Lowest tier. Seat No. 18." It was issued for the amphitheatre at Frosinone, but those of the Colosseum were quite similar and this one may admit us there. We will take the seat it calls for.

The arena, which has been strewn with dry sand to absorb the blood that will soon flow, glitters with gold and silver dust profusely scattered to increase the costliness of the display. The spectacle opens with a procession of those who will take part in the contests. Bands of Roman gladiators, groups of strangers, Parthians, Britons, Moors, Germans, each in his native costume and armed as he will fight, march to music around the arena. As they pass the throne, the gladiators address the emperor: " Hail, Cæsar! Those about to die salute thee." When the arena has been cleared, two trained athletes enter it and face each other. One is armed with a sword and shield. The other carries a light net, a dagger, and a tripod or three-pronged spear. The swordsman advances. The net-bearer draws back, turns and flies. The swordsman pursues. Inch by inch the fugitive gains till clear of danger. Suddenly his strength appears to fail. His pace slackens. The sword flashes over him. As it descends he leaps aside, and the weapon cuts the air. Before the swordsman can recover for a second stroke, the fatal net twinkles over him. A dexterous jerk throws him to the ground. He is helplessly entangled. The foot of the retiarius is upon him, the tripod pressed upon his breast. The victor glances upward at the "great cloud of witnesses," which "compass him about." If handkerchiefs are waved, he must spare, if thumbs are turned, he must slay. Thousands of women are watching. Among the 100,000 spectators not one lifts a finger to save life. Shouts of applause, clapping of hands, cries of "Kill! kill! kill!" salute the victor as he thrusts his triple spear again and again into the quivering flesh.

The single combats are succeeded by contests between bands of gladiators. The trained athletes of Rome are matched now against each other, now against foreign warriors, fighting according to the habits of their respective nations. Some are on foot, some on horseback, some in chariots. If any lag, they are driven forward by attendants armed with whips and bars of heated iron. During the interludes, boys dressed as Mercuries and Ganymedes, and girls as nymphs and dryads, bear about wine and ices and roasted fowls, — with the compliments of the emperor, — to regale the spectators, who chat, and gossip, and make love. A Roman poet declares that the amphitheatre was the chief place for match-making in Roman society.

The arena again is cleared; but the people remain seated. Suddenly the vast floor appears as if shaken by an earthquake. It sinks here, it bulges there, it yawns yonder. One knows not how, no theatre in existence to-day could do the same, a lake appears in the centre. Elephants are trumpeting upon its brink. Rocks and trees rise out of the ground. Lions, panthers, Libyan tigers, are gliding, crouching, leaping, roaring, among them. Bands of men armed with spears and bows and swords advance to fight them. Five thousand wild beasts were slaughtered at the opening games of the Colosseum. How many men fell on that occasion we are left to conjecture.

These were the favorite amusements of Rome. The passion for them grew until an emperor turned gladiator, and Roman ladies, generally protected in iron cages, descended into the arena to kill brutes and murder men.

Every city of note in Italy had its amphitheatre, where at times such sports were practiced. But a subtle force has begun to work, unseen as God and equally omnipotent, — a force which will in time teach men to feel the worth of human life and the loveliness of pity. Hundreds of Christian martyrs must perish in these shows. Throughout the empire, when pestilence or famine frightens the people and sets them seeking to appease the anger of their gods, the cry will be heard, " The Christians to the lions ! " But the martyrs will not die in vain. Soldiers will begin to ask, " Why do these men and women rejoice in being killed, while we no longer can rejoice in killing them ? " As they gradually learn the answer to that question, a sentiment will be born, which in due time, when a Christian monk descends into the arena of the Colosseum and is torn in pieces trying to stop the combat, will impel the emperor to prohibit gladiatorial shows forever, and the people to acquiesce in the decree.

IV. Just beyond the south bounds of the great Forum, opposite the Julian Rostra, stood the temple of Vesta. The small circular shrine so often copied on mosaic breastpins, which stands in another quarter of Rome, was long mistaken for this temple. The excavation of the house in which the Vestals lived was completed in 1884. It has fixed the site of the temple, and also modified our conceptions of its priestesses. The statues exhumed with the names of Vestal virgins inscribed upon their pedestals represent them as august matrons, draped in rich attire, with expressions of sweet and dignified benignity.

The religion of Vesta was the deification of family life under the symbol of the hearthstone. The characteristic of the early Roman was his reverence for the family. He gained his great strength fighting in its defense. The Romans honored father and mother, and therefore, as was, for the same reason, the fact in Egypt and in China, their days were long in the land which the Lord their God gave them. Marital fidelity was the foundation of their character, and therefore they were powerful. When these loyalties ceased to rule her, Rome rapidly grew weak. To the simple worship of the hearthstone the idolatries of Greece were added. The Pantheon arose, a building as unlike other buildings as the conglomerate of religions it represented was unlike other religions. The exterior of the edifice appeared a rounded hill of gold, a domed rotunda, with diameter of nearly a hundred and fifty feet, springing from the ground, and lighted at the top by a single circular opening, through which the sky viewed from beneath seemed a blue eye. The vast structure was neither stone, nor brick, nor iron, but cast in solid concrete. Without, the dome was covered with plates of gilded bronze. The interior, faced with variously colored marbles and frescoed stucco, contained niches for innumerable idols. One of these niches was offered for a statue of Christ. This was the building which Michael Angelo declared worthy to be translated, when he lifted its duplicate into the sky upon stupendous piers to form the dome of St. Peter's.

No nation has ever risen above its religion. Rome sank rapidly with hers. The vilest cult of the ancient world was that Syrian sun-worship with one form of which Jezebel inoculated Israel in the age of Elijah. It had long been creeping insidiously into Rome when, 219 years after Christ, the Emperor Elagabalus, a Syrian priest of the sun, planted it conspicuously there. He erected a superb temple upon the Palatine. Thither he carried the black stone symbols. They were displayed in a golden car. The priests of the old Roman gods followed, bearing their sacred emblems to be prostrated before the new divinity. The mysterious Palladium, which had always been concealed from public view, was ostentatiously exposed as his bride. The most illustrious men of the empire were compelled to join in the procession. The emperor on foot and clad in silk, a material counted so effeminate that no Roman ruler had ventured to wear it before, danced to the music of lutes, and whirled in fantastic attitudes, clashing cymbals before the idol. Syrian women wreathed lascivious figures around the shrine, and rites were practiced which cannot here be named. Human sacrifices emphasized the fact that cruelty and lust are twins. Thus the worship of the sun was established in the capital. That this marks one of the important events in the history of Christianity will presently appear.

From the day of Pentecost the new faith had been quietly leavening the empire. For a generation it received no hindrance but constant help from the imperial government. When its roots had grown strong enough to endure the storm, the persecutions began, and rapidly increased its strength. Against tremendous oppositions it had permeated every province, but had nowhere acquired a legal status when the sovereignty of the world was divided between the two emperors Constantine and Licinius. Constantine was a pagan, educated to worship the god of the sun. But he had seen much of Christianity, and been impressed by what he had seen. Two miles north of Rome, the Tiber was spanned by a bridge called the Milvian. There was fought the battle which made Constantine sole emperor of the West. In a march before the battle, if we may believe Eusebius, who declares he received the narrative from the emperor's own lips, a cross had appeared in the sky, *above the sun*, a little after midday, inscribed: " By this, conquer." The appearance was visible to the whole army. The next night Christ appeared to him in a vision displaying the same symbol and bidding him make it his standard.

Constantine obeyed. Then was fought the battle which made him the sole emperor of the West. The story is believed by high authorities; is doubted by high authorities. Some have attempted to explain it by natural causes acting upon an excited imagination. Some pronounce it wholly incredible. Some accept it as a miracle. But what follows none deny.

Constantine professed himself a Christian. Those who sympathized with that faith rallied to his support. Licinius was emperor in the East. To him the pagans turned for leadership 323 A. D., the two armies met in the battle of Adrianople. Pagan priests, soothsayers from Egypt, Arabian and Babylonian sorcerers thronged the army of Licinius. All the enchantments known to the heathen world were employed to insure the victory of Licinius.

The army of Constantine advanced beneath a standard called, we know not why, The Labarum. It was a spear made a cross. From the transverse beam hung a banner of silk, embroidered with portraits of Constantine and his family. On the summit of the cross rested a golden crown, inclosing an image of the cross marked with the monogram of Christ. The standard was guarded by fifty young men, the most illustrious in the army. Their office was believed to render them invulnerable to the arrows of the enemy. On the shields and helmets of the soldiers the cross was emblazoned, and the same emblem adorned the armor of the emperor. "*By this sign thou shalt conquer.*"

Constantine won the battle, and became sole ruler of the empire. In constituting Christianity the religion of the state, with deep insight he discerned the importance of the Lord's Day, and with a sagacity equal to his insight, in the decree for its observance upon the day sacred to the sun, no reference was made to our Lord's resurrection, but the day was still called Sunday. The sun-worshipers were very numerous. They recognized in Constantine their head. Would they not accept Sunday as a new honor to their own divinity, while Christians welcomed with delight legal protection of the time they had long been accustomed to hallow? The details of the required observances, among which were the enforced suspension of labor, especially of slave labor, and the interruption of public games, cordially received by Christians, might be acquiesced in by the pagans as new requirements of their god. Could they fail to appreciate the beneficence of the day, even before they understood its significance? Thus it would become a potent factor in destroying the religion they expected it to foster.

Such was the ultimate result of that frenzy of crime by which Elagabulus established in Rome the worship of the sun. From the dung heap which threatened to asphyxiate mankind, grew a tree of life-bearing leaves for the healing of the nations.

Very recently, in 1884, excavations determined the probable site of that bronze equestrian statue of Constantine holding the cross before the citizens of Rome, which was erected by his command. It stood in front of the temple of Vesta. It was appropriate that the emblem of all nobility should find its first resting-place in Rome beside the symbols of that religion of the hearth-stone which, though inadequate, had kept Rome noble so long as Rome remained noble! It was even more appropriate that the throne of Him who told us to take low seats if we would be exalted should, when removed from Calvary, be placed in the valley, at the foot of the Capitol it had subdued.

XI.

SAMARIA, THE CITY OF POLITICIANS.

THE word Samaria has two meanings. In the Old Testament it signifies the capital city of the ten tribes after their secession. In the New Testament it represents the central district of Palestine, which lay between Judæa and Galilee.

The separate history of the ten tribes begins with the year 985 B. C., which followed the death of Solomon, and ends B. C., 721, when they were carried into captivity by Sargon. For the first fifty years of this period, their capital was at Shechem or Tirzah.

I. Before the close of Napoleon's career, the French people began to realize with disgust that La Gloire, though a very fine thing, was vastly more prolific in death and taxes than in meat and drink. At the end of Solomon's reign, the Hebrew nation had long been smarting under a similar experience. No office in the kingdom required greater tact for its successful administration than that of tax collector, in the haughty tribe of Ephraim, for Ephraim still regarded itself as the divinely selected head of the nation defrauded of its rights by the house of David. To this difficult office Solomon appointed the young Jeroboam, who performed its duties so adroitly as to win the affections of the tax-payers without abating their taxes. The king soon perceived that his officer was too able for a subject. Jeroboam fled to Egypt, where he married a relative of the reigning monarch. Upon the death of Solomon, the fugitive returned to his own country, placed himself at the head of the popular discontent, and drew ten of the twelve tribes into secession. To win support from the religious classes, he posed as the champion of orthodoxy, and posed so well as to deceive, for a time, the very elect. With no principles but ambition, and no weapons but flattery, he was the ablest of pure demagogues mentioned in Old Testament history. To allure the more devout among his countrymen, he located his capital at Shechem.

A little north of the line along which the rugged hills of Judæa soften into the gentler terrace-like slopes of Ephraim, lies an upland plain. Its western boundary is formed by a sweep of hills shaped like a pair of recumbent sugar-tongs, with claws pointing east. The south claw, a precipice 800 feet high, is Mount Gerizim; the north claw, distant about 1,500 feet, and similar in shape and size, Mount Ebal. In the valley between them, clasped like a lump of sugar, though situated a little above the claws, toward the bend of the bow, lay Shechem. Before the building of the temple at Jerusalem, Shechem was a Mecca to the Jews. There Abraham had set up his first altar in the Holy Land. There Jacob had dug the well upon whose curb, long afterwards, Jesus sat wearied with his journey, and told the amazed woman of Samaria "all that ever she did." There Joseph was buried, and from the overlooking cliffs Joshua had promulgated the national constitution. At this spot, therefore, the sagacious demagogue, who knew the people followed him because they hated to pay their taxes, and wanted help in feigning nobler motives, fixed his capital, and announced himself the purifier of the national religion from the idolatries of Solomon.

He soon discovered that he had overreached himself. The memories of Shechem were the common heritage of the Jewish race, and its associations drew the seceders back toward their brethren and the worship at Jerusalem. The religious unity of the nation must be destroyed, or its political rupture would soon be healed, and Jeroboam crushed in the closing chasm. To prevent this, the schemer inaugurated a new ceremonial. He erected two golden calves, one at Dan, another at Bethel, copied from Egypt, and declared them the duly accredited emblems of Jehovah, similar to those made by Aaron in the wilderness. If the people had been familiar with their own history, a trick so transparent would have excited only contempt. But as the past was accurately known to very few, and the majority knew that Aaron had made a calf, and knew little more about the matter, the example of Moses's brother could be cited with effect. Like other demagogues, Jeroboam built upon the popular ignorance. Intelligent and conscientious men forsook his cause when this disguised idolatry appeared. They left Israel in large numbers, and removed to Judah. For this reason he was obliged to ordain as priests, ignorant and venal men, who depraved the people they should have elevated, propagated the lies they were told to teach, and prepared the way for all the misery that followed. This is the origin of that scathing epithet which rings through the later history of Israel, "Jeroboam, the son of Nebat, who made Israel to sin." His sin was the sin of all who see in religion their servant, not their master. For twenty-two years Jeroboam's great ability gave his shifty tricks an appearance of success. Two years after his death, the people, made by him poorer, more idolatrous, and vastly more unruly, because more ignorant, than he had found them, ended his dynasty by murdering his son, and embalmed his memory in perpetual execration.

II. The vacant throne was instantly seized by a usurper named Baasha, who anticipated the policy adopted by the United States in the Mexican war, and strove to establish his power, and divert public attention from internal dissensions by fixing it upon his attempted conquest of Jerusalem. But the blister did not cure the fever. A brave soldier and an able captain, Baasha retained the sceptre twenty-four years. Two years after his death his card-house fell, and his dynasty ended in the assassination of his son.

III. The army had now become to Israel what in a later age the Prætorian guard became to Rome. They made their captain, Omri, king. Though a soldier, Omri devoted his energies to the arts of peace, and strove to aggrandize the nation by increasing its wealth. As Jeroboam had appealed to avarice, and Baasha to pride, Omri built upon the common love of luxury and display.

A few miles north of Shechem, rimmed by an unbroken line of hills, lies a circular plain, extremely fertile, and six miles in diameter. In the centre of the plain an oblong mound slopes gently upward to a height of three hundred feet. This mound King Omri purchased and built upon it a new capital which he called from the name of its former owner, Shomer's Town, or Samaria. Its shape is suggestive. It lay stretching east and west like a giant's grave, covered with flowers. In it the nobility of Israel was buried beneath a pall of Tyrian purple.

Samaria was more easily defended than

Shechem, and more accessible to the lines of traffic between Tyre and Damascus. Without a care for the religious culture of the people, Omri established quarters in the new city for the merchants of Damascus, and apparently cultivated those commercial relations with Tyre which were consummated in the marriage of his son Ahab with a Tyrian princess. That marriage marks the beginning of a moral pestilence in Israel similar to that inroad of French infidelity which, after the Revolution, almost destroyed the faith of New England. The way had been well prepared. The ten tribes had been separated from the source of true religion at Jerusalem by the arts of a demagogue who debauched their conscience to wean them from their faith. The separation had been completed by unprovoked attacks of Baasha upon Jerusalem. Omri finding the nation practically atheistic, had taught it to worship wealth, when the splendor of Tyre began to fascinate Israel, as Paris once cast her spell over America. Her conscience debauched, her religion gone, her tastes tantalized by contact with a luxury she longed to share, Samaria opened her gates to receive a queen from the most sumptuous of existing courts. That queen was a woman of immense ability, with a strength and energy of character equaled by no other sovereign of the land she came to rule. Great-aunt of Dido, the foundress of Carthage, and daughter of Ithbaal, a high priest of Astarte, who gained the throne by murdering his master, she belonged to a line of religious fanatics, which neither fear nor pity ever swerved from its designs. She was the bravest and the cruelest of them all. Intensely sincere in her faith, resolved that whatever fell the worship of Baal should stand, the beautiful Jezebel entering Samaria to contend with Elijah reminds us of Mary of Scotland when, trained in the court of the terrible De' Medicis, she landed in Scotland to battle with John Knox.

Tyre was the principal centre of that sun worship which cast its baleful shadow over the whole ancient world. Originating in the land of Ur, in a noble admiration of the source of light, in Syria at last it rooted itself in the two most degrading passions of our nature, cruelty and lust. As the sun gave life, he must receive life in return. At first he was worshiped without images. Later, meteoric stones, which appeared to be shot in fire from his substance, and were believed to contain souls, were placed in his temple. Gradually he came to be figured as a man seated upon a bull; his hands full of fruits and flowers, his brow crowned with an aureole of gold rays, to symbolize the sources of fertility. Finally, he stood a brazen horror, with bull's head and arms extended to receive the little children which, placed upon the monstrous palms, glided through the gaping jaws into a furnace glowing within the idol's belly. Mothers who offered their little ones must not weep nor sigh, lest the god should be displeased, and reject the sacrifice. Flutes and trumpets drowned the children's cries, lest Baal or Moloch — for they were the same — should hear them and be angry. The Ganges seems merciful in comparison with this. Decency forbids description of the rites with which the consort of Baal was adored. Their shamefulness was scarcely equaled by the cruelties practiced in honor of her lord.

Authorities differ regarding the stage of development reached at Tyre by this cult. That city was long the chief centre of the system. Human sacrifices were common there. The Greek story of the Minotaur devouring fair maidens and slain by Theseus perpetuates the memory of this Phœnician worship and its overthrow in Crete. It is certain that human sacrifices were common in the colonies planted by Tyre, and the execration felt by the prophets of Jehovah for the religion of Jezebel is best explained by the probable hypothesis that it lacked but little of the extreme development it is known to have reached elsewhere.

Jezebel believed her religion with a strength of conviction, and practiced it with an energy of devotion, equaled by only one of her contemporaries, her great antagonist.

Her husband Ahab was a cipher. She was sovereign. When the king coveted a landed property which he could not buy and dared not steal, he whined, took to his bed, and sulked like a spoiled child. When Jezebel found him thus she said to him: "Arise, and eat bread, and let thine heart be merry: *I will give thee the vineyard of Naboth the Jezreelite.*" Instantly she convened the court, arraigned Naboth for treason, had him condemned and executed under forms of law, and had his possessions transferred to the crown.

Upon the queen's arrival a magnificent

temple to Baal was begun and soon completed in Samaria, and four hundred and fifty foreign priests appointed to administer its gorgeous ritual. But the summer palace built by Ahab became the favorite court residence.

The most beautiful and productive plain in Palestine lies but a few miles north of Samaria. From Mount Gilboa, curving south, the north line of the Samaritan hills runs west-northwest for eighteen miles, and terminates at the Mediterranean, in the promontory of Carmel. Northward from Gilboa a second range extends fifteen miles to Mount Tabor. Thence the south line of Galilean hills runs twelve miles, passing Nazareth, and reaching the sea a little north of Carmel. In the rich triangular plain inclosed between these ranges, near the foot of Gilboa, twelve miles east of Carmel Cliff, and distant seventeen from Samaria, lies a mound of earth very similar to that of Samaria itself, except that it is not quite so high nor so regular, and its east end terminates in a precipice of a hundred feet. This mound was named Jezreel, and after it the surrounding plain was called Esdraelon, which is Greek for " the plain of Jezreel."

Here Ahab built for Jezebel a sumptuous residence. The palace was so lavishly adorned with ivory as to be called "the ivory house." Here was built a second temple to Astarte, the consort of Baal, whose four hundred priests were entertained at the queen's own table.

Fascinated by the seductive though degrading allurements of the new religion, the people at first received it gladly. They soon felt the iron hand within the velvet glove. Jezebel would not rest until she had exterminated the worship of Jehovah. The priests and worshipers of the old faith were hunted and slain, till it seemed that not one was left. The new religion appeared to be firmly established. Its ministers thronged the capital. The queen had accomplished her purpose, when suddenly there appeared before Ahab, probably amid the court revels at Jezreel, a stern, wild figure, clad in a mantle of untanned skins caught about the waist with a leather thong. He entered the royal presence alone, uttered the single sentence, "As the Lord, the God of Israel, liveth, before whom I stand, there shall not be dew nor rain these years, but according to my word," and vanished. No one could tell whence he had come or whither he had gone. It was Elijah the prophet. The remainder of Ahab's reign was a duel between the man of God and the woman of Baal. Fidelity to facts will compel us to recognize that if the duel was not a drawn battle, Elijah did not win the victory. His career seems intended to teach the lesson effectually taught to him at last, lesson by receiving which he prepared the way before Christ, and earned the place upon the shining mount beside the Saviour, that not in the storm, and not in the lightning, but in the still small voice lies the power of God; that violence cannot establish the kingdom of Him who is a spirit, and must be worshiped in spirit and in truth.

Alone in the strength of his faith the prophet faced the court, the monarch, the people, the priests of Baal, more terrible still the awful queen, and threatened them with the wrath of Jehovah. Three years of deadly drought, the memory of which is preserved in the Tyrian annals of Menander as well as in the Bible, brought the timid Ahab and the fickle people suppliants to Elijah's feet. He demanded opportunity of testing whether Jehovah or Baal was God. You are familiar with the scene that ensued.

On the eastern crest of Carmel — the spot is accurately known — the king, the court, and the multitude were assembled. The 450 priests of Baal were before them. In plain view upon the west lay the Mediterranean, the water-way of Tyre. Conspicuous across the plain upon the east glittered the temple which proclaimed the general apostacy. Let this day prove who is God.

The revolution which followed the victory of Elijah was sudden as it appeared to be complete. The priests of Baal, 450 in number, were executed upon the spot, Ahab approving and the multitude applauding. The fugitive of yesterday became the autocrat of to-day.

In her palace at Jezreel the queen awaited intelligence from the contest. It came upon the lips of her husband. It told her that the prophets in whom she trusted were slain, the work of her life destroyed, the fickle people gone over to Elijah, her husband humbled before him, her life in peril from the revolution. Instantly the indomitable woman — every inch a queen despite her wickedness — sent word to Elijah in the hour of his victory, " So let the gods do to me, and more also, if I make not thy life as the life of one of them by to-morrow about this time." When Elijah received the message, "he arose and went for his life." He had treated the king as a silly child, he had met troop after troop of soldiers sent to apprehend him, and brought foes to their knees by a word or a gesture; he had stood alone against the priests with the king and the nation behind them, but he fled at the threat of Jezebel. He fled to the wilderness, and there received that revelation which leavened the spirit of Hebrew prophecy by teaching it to look for God, neither in the whirlwind nor the storm, but in the still small voice. As Jezebel had slaughtered the prophets of Jehovah, and seen her apparent victory melt into defeat, so Elijah slew the prophets of Baal only to experience the same result. Centuries later the Saviour, passing through Samaria, was received with scorn by its inhabitants. The disciples, perhaps reminded by the sight of Carmel of Elijah calling down fire upon the soldiers of Ahaziah, asked permission to imitate that prophet's example. But the Master rebuked them. "Ye know not what spirit ye are of."

Elijah gave place to another prophet, whose

spirit was to his in some small degree as the spirit of Jesus was to that of the Baptist. On the same mountain where Elijah wrought the fiercest deed recorded of any prophet of Jehovah, Elisha met the mother coming to tell him her son was dead, and followed her to perform the tenderest. There the old dispensation ended and the new began. Elijah vanished and Elisha appeared. Touches of cruelty appear in the career of Elisha, as touches of tenderness are shown in that of Elijah. But the later prophet, counted by most historians the inferior, we are compelled to esteem immeasureably the greater of the two if we believe the words of Him who came not to destroy men's lives, but to save them. For Elisha's history is the history of one who went about doing good in the spirit of Him who bade us love our enemies, and do good to them that persecute us.

IV. The last important stage in the rush of the nation toward ruin was the attempt of Jehu to rule by a pretense of religious reformation. A skillful soldier, an adroit and treacherous politician, his duplicity enabled him to retain the confidence of the reigning dynasty while he prepared to destroy it.

The instant rebellion appeared practicable, Jehu hastened at the head of the troops intrusted to his command by a confiding sovereign and seized the throne at Jezreel. The queen watched his approach from the window of her palace. His purpose was revealed by the detention of the messengers sent to ask his errand, and the murder of the king who went forth in confidence to welcome him. Jezebel was an aged woman, but indomitable still. Disdaining flight, she arrayed herself in the splendors of royalty and calmly waited for the traitor. As he drew near she said to him, in words which recalled the swift punishment of a former regicide in Israel, and were at once a threat and a command, "Had Zimri peace who slew his master?" Exasperated by her fearlessness or afraid of her influence if he spared her life an hour, he commanded the eunuchs in attendance to throw her from the window.

With her the dynasty of Omri fell. It had been preserved so long, not by the worldly wisdom of its founder, whose only conception of national prosperity was successful trade, but by the energy of a woman supremely wicked, but supremely able because she believed with all her heart and soul and mind and strength that her wickedness was the will of her gods.

Jehu committed the mistake usually made by men who have no principles when they try to imitate those who have. Despite the slaughter by Elijah, the Tyrian religion had again grown strong. Jehu copied the methods of Jezebel without possessing a trace of the spirit for Jehovah which had animated her for Baal. By a succession of treacheries unparalleled in any professed follower of Jehovah — exterminating on charges of heresy all who stood in the way of his ambition — he sustained himself in power for twenty-eight years. He is the earliest Jewish king whose name has been discovered in Assyrian inscriptions. On the black obelisk in the British Museum the ambassadors of Jehu appear with faces distinctively Jewish and wearing mantles fringed like that garment whose "hem" the woman touched when she was "straightway healed of her plague." They are bearing tribute to Shalmaneser and laying their master's sceptre at his feet.[1]

---

[1] It would be rash to defend the wickedness of Jehu by quoting his divine commission. David also was, dur-

With the exception of a single reign, that of Jeroboam II., when the exhausted forces of the nation flickered like a dying candle into temporary brilliancy, the remaining history of the ten tribes is a quagmire of idolatry, debauchery, treason, and murder, accurately indicated in the prophet's lament that no one could teach Samaria or steady the drunkards of Ephraim, where all tables were full of vomit so that there was no place

ing the life of his sovereign, anointed by divine authority. But David did not understand that he was meant to seize the throne by treachery and murder. The words addressed to Jehu by the messenger sent by Elisha to anoint him cannot be fairly attributed to Elisha, with whose character they are incongruous. What the messenger was *told* to do was to take Jehu into an inner chamber, anoint him, say "thus saith the Lord, I have anointed thee to be king over Israel," and *then* open the door and flee away and tarry not. What the messenger *did* was to say what Elisha had bidden him, and *then* a good deal more quoted from Elijah, but applied as a rule of conduct to Jehu by no other apparent warrant than the messenger's own. To justify his atrocities Jehu afterwards appealed not to the authority of Elisha but to that of Elijah, by whom it appears he was not anointed. That there was at some time of Jehu's career a spark of worthy impulse is implied though not necessarily indicated by the promise that four generations of his family should possess the throne. 2 Kings x. 30. But whatever of approval may be inferred from this and other passages is overbalanced by the weight of censure pronounced in the first chapter of Hosea.

clean. In 721 B. C. they were swept out of human sight forever and a strange people planted in the land they had defiled. What became of them no man knows. But their history with the attendant warnings uttered by inspired prophets against the sins which caused their ruin forms the most valuable statesman's manual that exists, for it contains in miniature the rise, progress, and results of all those dexterous devices by which politicians who are not statesmen endeavor to win or to perpetuate their power. The age of Elisha gave birth to that noble prophetic poem upon which small critics are accustomed to pour their frivolous contempt, but which stands without a rival, absolutely at the head of Old Testament literature, because it is most completely pervaded with the spirit of Christ, the book of Jonah. Who wrote the book named Jonah or "The Dove" we do not know. Whether the poem embodies the facts of some prophet's visit to Nineveh is uncertain. But here the poem stands and has stood for more than twenty-five centuries boldly proclaiming a statesmanship braver and more Christian by far than any statesman living or dead, pagan or Christian, has yet dared to practice or even to defend. For the book applies to all nations without reserve, even to nations which are threatening one's own land with destruction, the master's command, "Love your enemies; do good to them that persecute you." While Israel was bleeding from wounds dealt by foreigners, while the awful shadow of Assyria the destroyer was stealing nearer and nearer to blight his fatherland, an Israelite wrote the book which teaches that the men of Nineveh are as dear to God as the men of Israel, and that the sins which threaten to destroy Assyria grieve the heart of God no less than those which are corrupting Samaria. Shall we suffer the voice of a book which proclaims such doctrine to be silenced in our ears by brainless twitter about the size of fishes' throats and the length of time men may live beneath the water?

XII.

SUSA, THE CITY OF THE SATRAPS.

Susa, the Shushan of Scripture, was situated almost directly east of Babylon, and north of the present mouth of the Tigris and Euphrates. It stood upon a rich bottom between the Kerkhah, the ancient Choaspes, and the Dizful, the ancient Koprates, at a point where those rivers approached within three or four miles of each other. At the beginning of its authentic history, Susa appears as a place of great, though shadowy renown. The capital of Elam, it rivals in antiquity the oldest cities of Chaldæa. The annals of Assur-bani-pal inform us that the king of Elam invaded Babylonia more than two thousand years before Christ, and carried away the sacred images from Erech as trophies of his victory. By the Greeks, Susa was sometimes called Memnonium, as the reputed home of Memnon, the mythical hero who fought for Priam in the Trojan war, and who seems in classic story to be identified with an Ethiopia in Persia.[1]

The city comes distinctly and curiously to view about the year 650 B. C. Assur-banipal, the Sardanapalus of Greek story, was then king of Assyria. His annals are written upon cylinders found by Mr. Loftus. They bring before us the conqueror drawn by four captive kings, who are harnessed in chains before his war chariot, dragging it through the streets of Nineveh. He had come from the conquest of Susa, and one of the captive monarchs was its king. The annals give a minute account of the conquest

---

[1] The recent startling discovery by M. Dieulafoy is known to me only by the report in the *American Journal of Archæology*. In the most ancient part of Susa, M. Dieulafoy reports that he has found portions of a panel of enameled bricks, representing a king, "richly dressed in a green robe, overlaid with yellow, blue, and white embroidery, and in a tiger's skin; and carrying a golden cane or lance. The most singular point is that the figure, of which I have found the lower part of the face, the beard, neck, and hands, is black. The lip is thin, the beard abundant, and the embroideries of the garments, most archaic in character, seem to be the work of Babylonian workmen." M. Dieulafoy, it is added, recognizes in this black king of Susa the characteristics of the Ethiopian race, and thinks the picture older than any other relic yet discovered in the region. *American Journal of Archæology*, January and March, 1886.

and destruction of the city, and tell us that its tower or citadel was "laid in marble" and "the top covered with shining bronze."

Upon an alabaster panel placed by Assurbani-pal in the palace of his grandfather, Sennacherib, was sculptured the picture of an Elamite city inscribed "Madaktu." Mr. Loftus upon his return from excavating the mounds of Susa identified it as the map of that city without knowing that Mr. Layard had already done the same. The citadel, the palace, the royal gardens, the river, and the quarters of the common people all appeared in the positions assigned them in the diagrams of Mr. Loftus. It was startling to find, after excavating the naked mounds which conceal the ruins of Susa, a representation of the living city which had been carved on the panel of an Assyrian palace twenty-five centuries before. But the word "Madaktu" needed explanation. Mr. Layard thought it the name of the district in which Susa stood, and both he and Mr. Loftus called attention to the fact that an inscription on the adjoining slab states that the Assyrians defeated the Susians "near the district of Madaktu, and near the city of Shushan." Dr. Vaux inclined to believe "that the sculptor, himself probably an Assyrian, has, in error, called it 'Madaktu' instead of Susa."

The decipherment of Assur-bani-pal's annals has shown that Madaktu and Susa were separate cities and that the identification of the map was a mistake. But that the mistake occurred is a fact of great interest, because it shows the similarity in plan and structure of the Elamite cities, and so confirms other conclusions which have been drawn from their supposed resemblance to each other.

The victories recorded in these sculptures from the palace of Sennacherib, and repeated in another set of slabs discovered by Mr. Rassam in the palace of Assur-bani-pal, were among the last won by Assyria.

Soon after the sculptures were executed, Babylon became the world's capital. During her short supremacy, Susa rose to be the second city in the empire, and Daniel, whose tomb, a modern structure, is still shown upon the bank of the Kerkhah near the ancient citadel, was probably for a time its governor. According to the Book of Daniel, the seer was at Susa when the vision of the He-goat advancing from the West appeared to him. Under Cyrus, Susa began to share with Persepolis the supreme position which had been successively held by Nineveh and Babylon, and retained it until reduced to insignificance by Alexander.

We will visit Susa in the year 479 B. C., when for nearly half a century it had been the chief city of the world.

Cyrus founded the Persian Empire. When he had conquered Babylon, sent Zerubbabel thence with a company of Jewish exiles to rebuild their temple at Jerusalem, and fulfilled the glowing predictions of Isaiah by a long career of uninterrupted conquests, he made Susa a royal residence. After his death the power and wealth of the empire continued to increase, until its limits extended far beyond those reached by Assyria, or even Babylon. They included a great part of India, the whole of western Asia, Egypt, Asia Minor, and most of the Ionian Islands. This vast domain Darius divided into provinces or satrapies. He appointed over each of them a ruler accountable to no one but himself, and thus earned the title given him, "The Great King," and "King of kings." Enormous revenues poured into his treasury. Gold and silver and precious stones became so abundant in his capital that Aristagoras, who appears to have visited the place and been dazzled by its splendor, told the king of Sparta that the man who conquered Susa might rival Jove himself in wealth and power. One of the monarch's beds — perhaps the bed on which his son and successor Ahashuerus lay that memorable night when, because the king could not sleep, "he commanded to bring the book of records of the chronicles, and they were read before the king" — rested on a frame of solid gold. Over its head twined a vine, also of solid gold, bearing clusters of emeralds, rubies, and diamonds, representing grapes, green, and red, and white. It was made by Theodore of Samos, said to have been the most celebrated goldsmith of antiquity. Here also apparently stood a golden plane-tree, from the hand of the same artist. Darius appears to have been the earliest coiner of gold and silver. The gold darics, named after him, each showed the figure of an archer with drawn bow, and those archers conquered both Athens and Sparta after they had successfully repelled every other assailant the "Great King" could send against them.

Eleven years before we shall enter Susa, Darius experienced his first humiliation. In

490 B. C. his army was shattered at Marathon. Enraged by that defeat, he spent the remainder of his life preparing to avenge it. Each day, we are told, a slave was required to keep his fury aflame by whispering in his ear as he reclined at table, "Remember Athens!" Before his death Xerxes, his son and successor, had been pledged to expiate his father's disgrace by the subjugation of Greece.

Classic history informs us that in the third year of his reign Xerxes assembled the satraps of the empire at Susa to complete arrangements for the contemplated invasion.

The Bible tells us that in the third year of his reign Ahasuerus convened the rulers of his provinces at Shushan.

Classic history informs us that in the seventh year of his reign Xerxes returned defeated to Susa, and sought consolation in the pleasures of the harem.

The Bible tells us that in the seventh year of his reign Ahasuerus, after the empire had been searched for its loveliest women, married Esther.

Classic history informs us that Xerxes drained his dominions to furnish and replace treasures squandered in unsuccessful war.

The Bible tells us that Ahasuerus allowed his prime minister to pass sentence of death upon a wealthy race among his subjects in order to swell the royal revenues, and that he " laid a tribute upon the land and upon the isles of the sea."

The length of time between the divorce and the marriage is explained by the events narrated by the Greek historians, and cuneiform scholars add, with entire confidence, that Ahasuerus is Hebrew for the Persian equivalent of the Greek word Xerxes.

Even a careless reader of the Book of Esther can scarcely fail to observe the change which appears in Xerxes' treatment and estimate of woman, between his repudiation of Vashti and his marriage to Esther. Vashti was his toy, Esther his friend and counselor.

Four years elapsed between the divorce and the marriage. During that period Xerxes' eyes and thoughts were occupied with Greece. The great convention at Susa, during which Vashti was repudiated for disobeying a degrading command given by her husband in a drunken whim, was followed by the most memorable campaign of history, the campaign of Thermopylæ and Salamis. When Xerxes returned to Susa, he had spent four years in contact, more or less immediate, with Grecian sentiment, and two in a thoroughly Grecian atmosphere.

Those Greeks whom the " King of kings " went forth so confidently to enslave appreciated, more correctly than any other men then living, the worth and influence of woman, and treated her with a more just consideration. The Greek Bible was chiefly composed of two sacred poems. One of them, the Iliad, was the memorial of a war waged by the noblest of their race to avenge the honor of an outraged husband. It told how ten years of woes and the ruin of the guilty nation had been caused by a wife's infidelity. The other sacred poem, the Odyssey, showed how ten years of woes had been converted into blessing by the mutual fidelities of a wife, a husband, and a son. Both poems present true women, not as the toys, but the companions and counselors of man. To this truth the Greeks alone among nations were still bearing witness. The most foolish of men must learn something from four years in such a school. Did not Xerxes learn how a Spartan woman had detected and taught the baffled Spartan men to understand the dexterous device by means of which a friend of Greece had sent early intelligence of the Persians' plans, and so had saved her country by her superior sagacity? Did he not see the husbands and fathers of those women who had sent them to battle with the injunction, "Return to us bearing your shields, or borne upon them," fighting as he had not conceived it possible for men to fight? His own soldiers were driven to battle by scourges of raw bull's hide, while a line of selected guards followed behind them with drawn swords to slaughter all who fled; but when the Three Hundred, immovable as the rocks between which they stood, held at bay his million, and though surrounded could not be conquered, he learned that Greeks fought thus because their women would not speak even to the son or husband who had shown his back to a foe. Before the battle of Salamis, a woman, Artemisia, Xerxes' own ally, stood alone in opposing the plan adopted by himself and approved by all his generals. That plan, pursued against her protest, ended in irreparable disaster. This woman fought so well at Salamis that Xerxes, watching from the brow of Ægaleos the destruction of his ships, exclaimed, "My men fight like women, and my women like men!" He was glad after that to follow her advice, for he had already been nearly ruined by rejecting it, and showed his appreciation of her wisdom by intrusting his sons to her care. Thus, when Xerxes returned to Susa and found Esther, he had been prepared to appreciate a noble woman, so far, at least, as a man so foolish and so selfish could be taught that lesson.

We have reached the year 479, and will follow the king to his capital.

A little east of the Kerkhah or Choaspes river stood a rectangular platform of earth and masonry, its length from north to south half its breadth. Walls of brick and stone clamped with iron inclosed a solid filling of earth and gravel. The surface, an area of sixty acres, undulated in elevations varying from forty to seventy feet above the plain, and the entire mass was threaded with drains and water conduits. This was the broad pedestal upon which, amid trees and gardens, the royal residences stood. Some such structure was probably the original of Nebuchadnezzar's celebrated hanging gardens. A little west, probably in the line of the western wall, and upon the river bank — the river channel has changed within historic times — on a smaller but higher platform, triangular in shape, stood the citadel. East of the palace platform lay the city, on a broad foundation elevated a few feet above the plain.

Northwest of the great central mound which lay between the city and the citadel, Darius erected a fourth platform similar to that occupied by the royal grounds, but higher, half the size and square in outline. Here, inscriptions found upon the pedestals of broken and long-buried columns tell us that Darius built and Xerxes occupied the palace I would have you visit. It was unlike any structure ever seen outside of Persia, and combined in itself characteristics of Egyptian, Assyrian, and Greek architecture. Not a trace of the edifice remains above the ground, yet, for reasons which it may be interesting to understand, something of its general appearance is known. The locations of one or two pedestals of columns were discovered by accident, but these were not sufficient to justify even a conjecture of the plan of the building. Mr. Loftus reflected that it was thought to have been built in the time of Darius, and very probably might have resembled another palace of that monarch of which the ruins are still standing at Persepolis. He assumed that the two buildings were duplicates. Acting upon that hypothesis, he started from one of the pedestals already excavated, ran his trenches with mathematical precision to the points where other columns must have stood if his theory proved correct — found every pedestal almost exactly where he expected it; found fragments of shafts and capitals similar to those at Persepolis, and so demonstrated that to reconstruct the palace of Susa we have only to modify that of Persepolis.

The ruins of the structure at Persepolis are meagre. Only the ground-plan with the positions and appearance of the columns is certain. Beginning with these, adopting what has been with extreme probability inferred by competent judges, noting the few differences in details which excavations have disclosed, but introducing no feature not justified by considerations which seem to me sufficient, I will describe the summer palace of Xerxes at Susa as I believe it appeared.

Elevated a few feet above the vast mound-platform already described was a rectangular floor paved with variegated marbles and measuring 350 by 250 feet, if we discard odd numbers. It was reached by a low marble terrace of steps, flanked with Assyrian sculptures. Upon each of three sides of this broad and beautiful floor stood a colonnade. The colonnades did not fence the sides along their whole extent, but occupied only their central portions and so left open the corners of the square. Each column in these three colonnades, of pale blue marble with fluted shaft and elaborate capital, rose sixty feet above the floor and was surmounted by two half-bulls facing in opposite directions, so that the ends of the roof beams rested in the hollows upon their backs. Instead of walls, curtains of diverse colors hung from silver rings inserted in the capitals.

Near the middle of the south line of the great marble pavement, and equidistant from the three colonnades, stood a square group of thirty-six columns similar to those already described, equidistant from each other and rising like forest trees. This group was roofed, and its sides were protected by curtains, like those upon the colonnades, which could be adjusted at pleasure to exclude the sun or admit the breeze. The colonnades were probably the waiting-rooms or antechambers, the central group of columns the throne room. Those seeking audience of the monarch would have to cross the open space between the colonnades and the throne room, a distance of sixty feet, in full view of armed guards, whose duty it was to arrest and remove for instant execution every one who crossed the court unsummoned, though it should be the queen herself, unless the royal sceptre was extended in token of pardon or reprieve.

The sculptures have furnished us a picture of Xerxes seated upon his throne. The colors can be supplied from classic sources. The throne, which resembles a high-backed chair, is set in a frame of gold. The monarch wears yellow boots with pointed toes not unlike those found upon the sculptured rocks of Asia Minor, crimson trousers, and a flowing mantel of purple embroidered with gold. Instead of a crown, a square cap, with a fillet of white spotted with blue, the royal colors of Persia and worn only by the king, rests upon his head. His right hand grasps the sceptre, a golden rod five feet long and topped with a golden apple. His left holds a gold goblet, and behind him an attendant stands with an enormous fan of feathers.

No walls intercept his view. To his left,

beyond the royal gardens, beyond the citadel, beyond the river, fringed with a broad belt of the fragrant iris which gave to the city its name Shushan, the Lily, and still grows in great abundance around its ruins, a vast sea of golden grain, dotted with islands of palm, orange, and lemon trees, stretches to a distant shore-line of blue mountains. Behind him and nearly on a level with himself, lie the old palace grounds and buildings. On the east from the base of his lofty lookout extends the city. There he may see men rushing wildly through the streets, throwing handfuls of dust into the air, rending their garments, and practicing all those demonstrations by which Orientals express grief and dismay. Unless his own musicians drown the cries, he hears the shrill screams, "Woe! woe! woe! woe to the sons of Abraham! woe to the children of Israel." For a decree has gone forth that all of Jewish lineage shall be slain, and while the palace of Shushan is at ease the "city Shushan is perplexed."

But the monarch's gaze is arrested by the figure of a woman crossing the open court toward the throne room. She is radiantly beautiful, and every art of the toilet has been employed to increase her beauty, for she knows it is the single thread upon which her life and the lives of her people depend. Therefore she has put on her royal apparel and advances shining in all the lustre of that loveliness which may have caused her name to be changed from Hadassah, the myrtle, to Esther, the star.

While we recall the immense results of that interview, let us not forget the experience which had educated Xerxes not only to admire the grace, but to appreciate the mind and character of a wise and noble woman.

Many scholars who do not regard the Book of Esther as authentic history, still think that it contains a picture, the most vivid and accurate that exists, of the Persian court in the age of Xerxes.

Without this book it is scarcely possible to account for the position occupied by the Jews in the Persian Empire, and at the court of Artaxerxes in the age of Nehemiah. Without it, Jewish annals between the first rebuilding of the temple and the work of Ezra and Nehemiah are a blank. At the accession of Artaxerxes only a small colony of the chosen people resided at Jerusalem. The vast majority of their race were still in exile. Many lived at Babylon, many at Susa. They held positions of influence and authority; they possessed great wealth, and some of them shared the counsels of the king. They thought of their brethren at Jerusalem somewhat as Englishmen thought of Massachusetts in early colonial times. It was Artaxerxes who sent Ezra from Babylon, and Nehemiah from Susa, with large reinforcements of men and treasure to reëstablish the Jewish nation. As Babylon was the destroyer, Persia was the savior of the chosen people, and from Susa came the influences which restored to the world, after they appeared to have been lost forever, not only Moses and the prophets, but the many other blessings inherited from Jerusalem.

The history of Persia was a long note, of which the career of Alexander was a brief answering echo. That history began in a mountain district which formed a smaller part of Asia than does Switzerland of Europe. With his hardy mountaineers Cyrus attacked whom he would, and no one was found who could stand before him. Rapidly he subjugated the countless nationalities of which he formed the great Persian Empire, and his successors were long able to sustain the greatness he had given them. When luxury and pride had completed their work, Xerxes invaded Greece with a host which the calm and judicial Grote allows us to estimate at nearly two millions, and made less permanent impression than foam upon a rock.

Two centuries later another mountaineer set forth to capture Susa. He had less than thirty-five thousand soldiers, but each of them had been trained to endure hardness, to trust his comrades, to choose death before defeat, and to obey orders. At Issus their way was blocked by 600,000, at Gaugamela by 1,000,000 armed men. Without checking its course, the phalanx plowed through them, sending the opposing hosts in fine spray, right and left, as a swiftly moving ship throws the jets from her cut-water. Pausing only long enough to gather the treasure dropped by Darius as he fled from Issus, and to return in safety to their lord the royal ladies there deserted; stopping at Tyre to fight real soldiers; at Jerusalem to confer with real men, and in Egypt to be told he was a god; halting while his general brought the chests of Persian treasure abandoned at Damascus; stopping scarcely long enough to count the gold captured at Babylon, Alexander advanced to Susa, where sixty million dollars awaited him, and Persepolis, where he found a hundred and thirty million more. Never has any other conqueror been opposed by armies so numerous, wealth so prodigious and manhood so feeble. It is scarcely strange that he believed himself a god, not because he was so great, but because other men were so little. Insatiable of conquest, he descended to India. There he found one who told him what these things meant. They meant, not that Alexander was a god, but something very different. Gods should be omnipresent in some small measure. To emphasize that fact, Calanus brought the shriveled bull's-hide, laid it before Alexander-Ammon, and trod upon its edge. Watch, O Alexander-Ammon, how the opposite edge flies upward.

That is all the sage, sought by the conqueror to flatter his vanity, will say. But the symbol declares sharply, "While you stand at Susa, take care for Macedon." Never was prediction more accurately fulfilled.

It is the last ten years of Alexander's life which seem like a short, sharp echo of the history of Persia. At twenty-three a noble youth, generous, brave, temperate, he left the shores of Greece. At thirty-three, corrupted by success and wealth greater than have ever been given in equal measure to any other of our race, whimsical as Xerxes, and debauched as Persian kings, he died at Babylon the drunkard's death.

The invasion of Alexander crushed the empire which Cyrus had founded. The influence of Greece superseding that of Persia permeated Egypt and the Orient. The cuneiform alphabet, though employed to some extent as late as the first century of our era, gradually fell into disuse, and even Chaldæan priests began to write in the language of the Macedonian. The empire of Cyrus endured two centuries, that of Alexander perished in a night. As the Hebrew prophet had distinctly foreseen, the important work of Cyrus and his successors was to replant, in its native soil, the vine which once had flourished at Jerusalem. The important work of Alexander was to prepare the way by which the fruits of that vine should be distributed among mankind. The commissions by which both conquerors were empowered we copy from the book of Isaiah. They read as follows : —

"Thus saith the Lord, . . . that confirmeth the word of his servant, and performeth the counsel of his messengers; . . . that saith of Cyrus, He is my shepherd, and shall perform all my pleasure: even saying to Jerusalem, Thou shall be built; and to the temple, Thy foundation shall be laid. Thus saith the Lord to his anointed, to Cyrus, . . . For Jacob my servant's sake, and Israel mine elect, I have even called thee by thy name: I have surnamed thee, though thou hast not known me. . . . That they may know from the rising of the sun, and from the west, that there is none beside me. I am the Lord, and there is none else."

"The grass withereth, the flower fadeth: but the word of our God shall stand forever. O Zion, that bringest good tidings, get thee up into the high mountain: . . . lift up thy voice with strength!"

XIII.

JERUSALEM, THE CITY OF THE PHARISEES.

THE present Jerusalem stands over the ancient city upon a mass of débris which varies between twenty and one hundred, and averages more than thirty feet in depth. But the original outlines are revealed in the overlying mould as the bones of a limb in the contours of the flesh. Within an area of two hundred acres, hundreds of observations of the old levels have been taken by means of shafts sunk to the bed rock, and galleries run in various directions. The conclusions reached have been tested by careful comparison with descriptions given in the Bible and by profane writers. It is, therefore, possible to realize with considerable accuracy and distinctness the appearance of the city in the time of Christ.

It was shaped like a two-pronged tooth, of which the crown was a projection from the south line of the Judæan hills, and the prongs extended southward. The west prong bulged westward, and the valley bounding it on the west and curving eastward around its point was called Hinnom. The depression between the prongs, shallower but steeper than Hinnom, was the Tyropœan, or Valley of the Cheesemongers. The valley which bounded the east prong on the east ran a very little east of south, entered the valley of Hinnom south of the east line of the city, and was named Kedron. From·their junction the three valleys ran as one eastward toward the Jordan. Irregularities of outline gave the city a shape which might suggest that of a diamond with the longer diagonal running from northeast to southwest. That longest diagonal was less than a mile, the circuit of the walls was less than three, and the area of the city, exclusive of the temple inclosure, was two hundred and ten acres.

The eastern ridge, or prong, was formed by three eminences. The south and lowest of these, which sloped upward from the junction of the three valleys, and lay outside the city walls, was Ophel. Upon it the palace of Solomon probably stood. The higher elevation, directly north of Ophel, with a dome-shaped crest, was Mount Moriah. A rectangle of enormous walls, varying in depth between thirty and a hundred and seventy feet, was built from the bed rock, at the base of the dome, to a level with its summit. The space between these walls and the hill they inclosed, filled in, formed the temple inclosure. It was nearly a mile in circuit, and a part, probably the greater part of the east side rising from the Kedron valley, was terraced with vines and flowers. North of Mount Moriah, separated from it by a sharp ravine, which is now filled up, defended by the city wall which surmounted a precipice, adorned with gardens, and occupied by residences of the wealthy, was Bezetha, or new town.

The western ridge was higher than the eastern. Due west of Mount Moriah, across the Tyropœan valley, which was the commercial centre of the city, it swelled into the rounded eminence called Acra. South of Acra and divided from it by a ravine, which is now filled up, and directly west of Ophel stood Mount Zion, the highest elevation in Jerusalem. It rose above the temple hill, more than a hundred feet.

On the crest of Zion, Herod the Great

erected the palace in which Christ stood before Pilate. It was of vast size, and built wholly of white marble. Some of its innumerable apartments were paneled and ceiled with variegated marbles, thickly set with precious stones. The banqueting hall afforded room for the couches of three hundred guests. The surrounding gardens covered the greater part of Zion. They were adorned with fountains and artificial watercourses, which leaped in cascades, or rested in ornamental fish-ponds, and were profusedly decorated with those pagan statues which exasperated the religious sentiment Herod built the temple upon Mount Moriah to appease. The whole palace grounds were inclosed by fortified walls, also of white marble, and forty-five feet in height. The city walls ran a little west of these, and near them on the north arose the three celebrated towers built by Herod, and named by him Hippicus, Phasaelus, and Mariamne. Each was at once a sumptuous palace and a fortified castle. They were built of blocks of white marble so deftly fitted to each other that their lines of junction were said to be scarcely visible.

We have named the most striking objects

in Jerusalem, when the Master viewed it the last week of His life. He was standing upon the Mount of Olives, which formed the east bank of the Kedron, and rose several hundred feet above the city. Directly beneath him lay the deep valley. Its sides were terraced with vines and flowers, and its surface covered with gardens, one of which was called Gethsemane. Across the valley the temple hill, crowned with buildings of dazzling white, surmounted with countless points of burnished metal, appeared "like a mountain of snow fretted with gold." A little farther west and south appeared the palace and gardens of Herod, flanked upon the north by the three gorgeous castles of white marble. Beyond this glittering centre, which might seem a jeweled broach, pinning to earth a variegated mantle, gardens, orchards, vineyards, extended far as the eye could see. They were thronged with hundreds of thousands of men, women, and children, moving about with the vivacity of their Christmas season, for it was the Passover, and more than a million visitors had come to celebrate the feast. This was the brilliant and inspiring view spread before the gaze of the disciples when the Master " drew near and beheld the city and wept over it." For he discovered, what in less than forty years other eyes should also see, every edifice in sight razed to the ground; of the temple buildings not one stone left upon another; the site they cover plowed, and the furrows sown with salt; every garden made a desert; every tree cut down; in the places of those which stand in Gethsemane, and of the vines which terrace the slopes of Kedron, hundreds of wooden crosses, and upon every cross one of his countrymen stretched in the agonies of crucifixion, while the sun is darkened by the vultures hovering over them. " O Jerusalem! Jerusalem!"

The Bible gives the history of Jerusalem from the day when David fixed his residence upon Mount Zion to the time when the Jews who had been sent back from Babylon by Cyrus with Zerubbabel to rebuild their temple began a new lease of national life under Ezra and Nehemiah. After that the Bible is silent until it begins to describe the birth of Christ.

The history of Nehemiah ends about 433 B. C. A century later Alexander received the Jews under his protection. They continued under Greek influence, shuttlecocked between Egypt and Syria for more than a century and a half. Gradually Greek manners crept into Jerusalem, until their insidious influence threatened to obliterate the religion of the chosen people. That result seemed near, when it was prevented by the violent endeavors of one man to accelerate it. Near the middle of the second century before Christ, Antiochus Epiphanes, a usurping and half-mad king of Syria, undertook to force the Jews to a complete renunciation of the religion they were gradually renouncing of their own accord. He was actuated in part by a brutal love of tyranny, in part by the hope of bringing Jerusalem into closer political relations with the rest of his dominions, through a community of faith, but chiefly by a desire to possess the immense treasures in the temple. He abolished the laws of Moses, prohibited their practice, desecrated the temple by offering swine's flesh upon the altar and setting up a statue of Jupiter in the Holy of Holies, and required every Jew to offer pagan sacrifice under penalty of death for disobedience.

At Modin, some miles from Jerusalem,

lived an old man named Matthias. He had retired, with his five stalwart sons, from Jerusalem to avoid sight of the profanations practiced there. When the Syrian official visited Modin to compel obedience to the edict of Antiochus, Matthias, seized with uncontrollable fury as he saw the pagan approach to consecrate the altar of idolatry, slew him on the spot. This murder inaugurated a revolution, which made the Jews once more an independent nation. Judas, named Maccabæus, or the Hammerer, a son of Matthias, become the Jewish William Tell, and his memory is still preserved as that of the only Jewish warrior who deserves to rank with Joshua. He defeated the armies sent against him, though they outnumbered his own ten to one. Under his rule, and that of his four brothers, the Jews retained their independence. Eventually, however, they were compelled to seek the alliance of Rome. That step prepared for the intervention of Pompey, who was asked to arbitrate between two rival claimants of the high-priesthood. Using the occasion to advance his own ambition, Pompey besieged and captured Jerusalem, 63 B. C. Thenceforth it remained nominally independent, but virtually a feudatory of Rome, until the birth of Christ. Soon after that it became nominally, as it had been virtually, a Roman province, and at the time of the crucifixion was governed by a Roman procurator.

The patriots who struck for religious liberty under Judas Maccabæus were the Puritans of Palestine. Their battle-cry was, "God and our native land." Their constitution was not only the Mosaic law, but the minutest details of the ritual observances which had been engrafted upon it. They were called " Pharisees," or " Separatists," to distinguish them from other Jews less scrupulous and less patriotic. Gradually they passed through that experience so vividly portrayed in Walter Scott's portrait of Balfour of Burleigh. Their religious and patriotic ardor petrified into an arrogant and cruel conceit. For the letter and external forms of their religion they stood like a rock. For its spirit they ceased to care a jot. In the time of Christ they had become the popular leaders, had inoculated the people with their own spirit, and were steadily urging them forward toward the hopeless struggle with Rome. They scrutinized Christ so long as they hoped he could be used as a military captain, a second Judas Maccabæus, and crucified him when they discovered their mistake. They were responsible for the horrors of the siege by Titus. The details of that siege are familiar. We will not repeat them. It is not needful to describe again famished parents feeding upon the bodies of their children, murdered by their own hands, and fighting each other for the fragments of the terrible feast. That siege was not only the most awful of the twenty-one recorded sieges of Jerusalem, but it greatly surpassed in horror any other known to history. The number of Jews who perished in it by famine and the sword is estimated at more than 1,100,000. Ninety-seven thousand were taken prisoners. "The entire nation," says Ewald, "was really by this siege affixed to the cross, only there was not wood enough at hand for such wholesale crucifixion." "Of the prisoners, some were obliged to slay each other as gladiators, or to be torn by wild beasts in the arena. Others were doomed to unwholesome labor as slaves in Egypt. And all Israelites without distinction were then with one blow made the scorn of the whole world, whilst only a short time before they had supposed that they had a right to despise or rule the world."

Nothing was left of the city but the naked hills, and the valleys between these were largely filled by the conquerors, to prevent their being fortified again.

The important memories of Jerusalem all rest upon the three hills, Mount Moriah in the eastern ridge, Zion and Acra in the western.

I. Mount Moriah, or the "Mount of Vision." Here the tradition accepted by Josephus, the Jewish Targums, and by some living scholars of repute, affirms that Abraham placed the wood upon which he meant to offer Isaac. Here, certainly, was the threshing floor of Ornan, where the devastating angel paused when the pestilence was arrested, and here David erected an altar to perpetuate the memory of that deliverance. Here, upon the inclosure already described, stood successively the temple of Solomon, the temple of Zerubbabel, and that built by Herod, in which Jesus taught. At the southeast angle of the stupendous walls which include the vast quadrangle surmounted by the temple buildings, and more than seventy feet beneath the present surface of the Kedron valley, from which those walls arise, lies the foundation stone. The great stone, fourteen feet long and three feet eight inches high, is sunk fourteen inches into the bed rock. It is sharply squared, polished, and finely faced. It was laid for Solomon, it is believed, three thousand years ago, and may have been in Peter's mind when he wrote, " Behold, I lay in Zion a corner-stone, elect, precious." Three feet from it, cut in the bed rock, is a small hole, a foot broad and a foot deep, in which was found a small earthen jar, which Dr. Birch recognized as of Egyptian, but which others think, with greater probability, of Phœnician pattern. It was probably filled with the holy oil of consecration, and placed by Solomon with imposing ceremonies in the place where the excavators found it, as a part of the ritual with which the foundations of the temple were laid. Directly above this corner-stone the top of the cloister wall rose in the time of Christ, three hundred feet sheer, and here was perhaps the spot referred to in the temptation, as " the pinnacle." Fifty yards north of the southeast angle, built into modern masonry, the fragment of a column projects over the Kedron, and upon it Mohammedans believe their prophet will sit when, on the last day, he returns for the last judgment, and all nations are gathered before him in the valley beneath. The entire temple hill is honey-combed with drains, water conduits, cisterns, of which last enough have been explored to contain 11,000,000 gallons, and chambers whose uses are not known. A shaft sunk outside the great walls near their southwest angle disclosed an ancient pavement, twenty-three feet below the present surface, and twenty feet beneath that a second pavement. There, amid fragments of pottery and glass, a gentleman's seal was found. It is about the size worn to-day in gentlemen's rings and is a finely grained black stone, inscribed " Haggai, the son of Shebnaiah." The letters resemble those employed during the age of the captivity in Babylon. The prophet Haggai was one of the exiles who returned with Zerubbabel. " He is," says Mr. King, "the only one of the minor prophets who mentions a signet," and one can imagine him holding the ring upon his finger before his leader's eyes, to emphasize the words which close the book of the prophecy which has come down to us under his name: "I will take thee, O Zerubbabel, my servant, the son of Shealtiel, saith the Lord, and will make thee as a signet; for I have chosen thee, saith the Lord of hosts."

A few years after the destruction of Jerusalem by Titus, Hadrian planted a Roman colony upon its site. He built a temple to Jupiter where the temple of Jehovah had stood, prohibited Jews from coming within sight of the place upon penalty of death, and called the city Ælia Capitolina. Two centuries later Constantine made Jerusalem the devotional centre of Christianity as it had once been of Judaism.

After a single intervening reign, Constantine was succeeded by the Emperor Julian. The aim of Julian's life was the overthrow of Christianity and the restoration of paganism. He recognized in the Jews the bitter opponents of the religion he wished to destroy. For that reason he recalled them to Jerusalem and encouraged them to rebuild their temple. They responded with fierce alacrity. They crowded Jerusalem. Day and night the work of reconstruction proceeded. All classes and ages were animated by a common enthusiasm. The rich worked with picks or spades of silver to emphasize their zeal. Wealthy ladies carried rubbish in mantles of silk and purple and in baskets made of silver. Old men and even the blind were led tottering among the ruins, and little children were carried by their parents and their hands filled with pebbles that all might share the blessings expected upon an enterprise so holy. Much of the rubbish had been removed, when suddenly, we are told by both Christian and pagan historians, the work was miraculously stopped. Flames burst from the ground, balls of fire shot through the air or rolled along the earth and exploded with a sound of thunder. The sign of the cross appeared on every side in fire. No historian of repute, I believe, has ventured to deny the reality of this mysterious interruption. The evidence is too overwhelming. We are able at last to explain its origin. The temple hill is honey-combed with caverns. The air long imprisoned within them had become explosive and phosphorescent, and when the sparks struck by pick or spade touched these reservoirs of imflammable gases, explosions ensued, and the high-wrought imaginations of superstitious men, ignorant of natural laws, completed the miracle.

In 637 A. D. the Saracens gained possession of the city. They raised the mosque of Omar on the summit of the temple inclosure, known as the Dome of the Rock. This highest point of Mount Moriah is called the Sakhra. It rises five feet through the marble pavement of the mosque, and the pavement itself is twelve feet higher than the surrounding surface of the hill. The Sakhra is perforated by an opening leading into the drain along which there is reason to believe the blood shed in Jewish sacrifices was conducted into the Kedron. It probably marks the spot where the altar to Jehovah stood. It is venerated by Mohammedans as the spot whence Mohammed ascended to heaven. The present building which covers it is a restoration of the structure built in the seventh century, and was made by Solyman the Magnificent.

When the crusaders captured Jerusalem in 1099 they erected upon Mount Moriah the buildings occupied by the Knights Templar.

It is the irony of history that for 1,500 years no Jew has been allowed to set foot upon this hill, on the summit of which it was in the time of Christ death for a Gentile to tread. The Jew may approach no nearer than the outer surface of the western wall. There, on payment of a sum of money, they have been permitted to come, and there they have come for centuries, and still come on stated days to kiss the hallowed stones, bewail the sins which have lost them the favor of Jehovah, and pray for the restoration of their holy ground.

II. But the western ridge of Jerusalem has for us a greater interest even than Mount Moriah.

Its southern eminence was called, as we have seen, Mount Zion, or "The Sunny." This was the ancient Jebus of which we read: "The inhabitants of Jebus said to David, Thou shalt not come hither. Nevertheless David took the castle of Zion, which is the city of David. And David said, Whosoever smiteth the Jebusites first shall be chief and captain. So Joab the son of Zeruiah went first up, and was chief." Here the ark rested before the building of the temple. Here Christ stood before Pilate in the palace which Herod had built. From its gardens Roman soldiers plucked the twigs of white-thorn and the reed for the mock crown and sceptre. From that hour Zion passed out of history to be embalmed in hymns and prayers.

The eminence north of Zion named Acra is believed to-day by very weighty authority to be Golgotha or Calvary, upon which the cross of Christ stood, near by the garden and the new tomb " wherein was never man yet laid." With the great authority of Dr. Robinson opposed to the identification, we venture to affirm only that 326 years after Christ the Empress Helena, the mother of Constantine, visited Jerusalem. Though she was eighty years old, her devotion burned with the enthusiasm of youth. She made diligent inquiry for the site of the crucifixion. She was shown this spot. It was at that time regarded as the true site of the Passion.

To banish all doubts, three crosses and a clay placard inscribed as that upon which Pilate wrote " Jesus of Nazareth, king of the Jews," were exhumed before the eyes of the empress.

When and by whom they were buried we scarcely need to ask. But whatever trickery may have been practiced tends to strengthen the force of the tradition, as the reputed site would naturally have been selected for the scene of its performance.

Few facts in history are so well authenticated as that here Helena believed she had found the cross of Christ and the place of the crucifixion and the resurrection. After paying her devotions here, she erected the Church of the Nativity at Bethlehem, and that of the Ascension upon Olivet. Her son Constantine built the first Church of the Holy Sepulchre. The story is that he found over the actual grave a temple to Venus. When this had been removed the cave was brought to view in which the body of Jesus had lain. The emperor cut away the surrounding rock, leaving only the walls of the cave, encased them in white marble, and erected over them a noble building. The English Ordnance Survey, which is high authority, declares that the appearance of the locality closely corresponds with the tradition.[1]

[1] "The sepulchre in which the body of our Lord was laid was originally a nearly square chamber of about six feet in length and breadth and about nine feet high. It lies nearly east and west; and on the north side there is a low bench, on which the body was laid. The entrance to the chamber was by a very low passage leading into the south side from the east. The sepulchre was cut into the natural rock, but when the Emperor Constantine, at the instigation of his mother Helena, determined to do honor to this sacred spot, he is said to have caused the rock all round the sepulchre to be cut away to form a

Beneath the temple of Constantine the cross remained, attracting innumerable pilgrims to worship it, until Jerusalem was taken by the Persians A. D. 614, the church destroyed, and the cross carried away. It was brought back by the Emperor Heraclius, who entered Jerusalem with an imposing procession of priests and warriors, bearing the cross upon his shoulders, and placed it again in a shrine rebuilt over the spot whence it had been taken. The crusaders found the site occupied by a small building with an open dome, and a chapel, one hundred and forty feet south of it, upon the reputed place of the crucifixion. They inclosed both structures in the noble church of which the principal parts still remain.

In 1099 the crusaders took Jerusalem by

spacious inclosure round it, leaving the sepulchre itself standing in the midst, and an examination of the ground fully sustains this description." *Ordnance Survey.* The site of Calvary is thirteen feet higher.

The difficulty which was urged by Dr. Robinson against this identification, and which appears insuperable, is that the locality almost demonstrably lies within the line of the ancient walls, and Christ was crucified "without the gate."

Professor Dawson thinks that a small elevation north of the city, which from certain directions bears some resemblance to a skull, is the true site.

storm. When they first caught sight of Zion, every soldier fell upon his knees and all voices joined in a hymn of praise. Before beginning the assault the rival leaders, Tancred and Raymond, who were at bitter feud, embraced each other in sight of all the army. The soldiers and other leaders followed their example. All swore to forget their discords and love one another for Christ's sake. Then they stormed the city. They entered it on Good Friday, at the hour when they believed their Master had prayed for his enemies, "Forgive them, Father." They began at once an indiscriminate massacre, which continued three days. They murdered in cold blood 70,000 defenseless prisoners. They tortured the infidels, roasted them before slow fires, ripped open the bodies of living men to discover if they had swallowed gold. The worst passions of our nature rioted not only unrestrained, but stimulated by religious zeal. Lust and cruelty and avarice were baptized in the name of Christ. For outrages inflicted on the infidels seemed to the maddened crusaders vindications of the honor of their Lord.

When wearied with slaughter, the whole Christian army marched in procession barefooted, bare-headed, up the hill of Acra, to the supposed sepulchre of Christ, kissed its stones, wet it with their tears, and gave thanks in hymns and prayers. Was this pure Phariseeism? It is but another proof of what history is perpetually teaching us, that no other sentiment has ever made men so devilish as religious zeal without the spirit of Christ.

For eighty-eight years the Christians held possession of Jerusalem. Then it was retaken by Saladin. His treatment of the captives affords a lovely contrast to the horrors perpetrated by the Christians in their hour of victory. From the conquest of Saladin, the Holy City has been almost continuously under Mohammedan control.

Probably no other battles fought on earth have shown so much bravery, such demoniac passion, and such relentless fury as those which have been fought for the possession of Jerusalem. For in most of its twenty-one recorded sieges the city has been defended and assaulted by men who believed themselves the especial favorites of heaven obeying the direct commands of God. Jew, Mussulman, and Christian, each has expected with equal assurance the miraculous intervention of God in his behalf. This conviction has made its defenders fight with a valor no language can exaggerate, and often with a cruelty which it is scarcely possible to credit. But the millions of soldiers who have perished for the honor of Jerusalem have added no feather's weight to its influence among mankind. It has ruled the world only because One who had long inspired its psalmists and its prophets wept over it, walked through its streets saying, "They that take the sword shall perish by the sword," "Love one another," gave his life in it for his enemies, died saying, "Father, forgive them," and rose again to shed his Spirit upon all flesh.

XIV.

NEW JERUSALEM, THE CITY OF GOD.

I.

DRIVEN from Jerusalem by the violence of their countrymen who had crucified Christ, the disciples went in all directions sowing the Saviour's teachings in soil prepared for its reception. To change the figure, the world was a vast prairie covered with dry grass. The crucifixion kindled a spark. The resurrection made the spark a flame. The murder of Stephen was the stamping of frightened men who, in trying to put it out, scattered a thousand new sparks, each of which started a new fire where it fell.

For more than a generation the Jews fought single-handed against Christianity. The Roman government sheltered the new faith from their fury and assured free course to its preachers. At the close of that period there was probably no considerable city in the empire where the gospel had not been heard, and few which did not contain believers. When the roots of the tree were set the storm came.

On the eighteenth of July, A. D. 64, a fire broke out in Rome. It originated among shops occupied by Jews near the great circus. It raged six days and seven nights, appeared to go out, burst forth again, and raged three days longer. The great fire at Chicago consumed less than a third of that city. The great fire at Rome consumed five sevenths of the place, and left the metropolis of the world in ruins.

Nero, the emperor, was at Antium, his seaside villa, when the fire began. On the evening of the third day he returned to Rome. He mounted the roof of Mæcenas' palace to view the conflagration. Excited to frenzy by the splendor of the spectacle, he called for his lyre, and in scenic dress chanted before applauding sycophants a description of the burning of Troy.

It was not unreasonably inferred that one so callous to the immeasurable calamity might be its author. The rumor gained credence that Nero had fired the city to clear the ground for a palace he wished to build. It was necessary to divert the popular fury to some other victim. Who should be made the scapegoat? Why not accuse the Christians of the crime? The charge would appear plausible. The fire had begun in the shops of Jews. The Christians were known as a Jewish sect at feud with the rest of their countrymen. The fire had destroyed the great circus, and the great circus was the conspicuous representative of those popular amusements which the Christians were known to abhor. The fire had destroyed every temple and nearly every idol in Rome. The Christians were known as enemies of the temples, and such was their hostility to idols that it was believed they would not touch a Roman coin because it bore the image of Cæsar, nor pass through a gateway surmounted by a pagan image. What was even more significant, the Christians had constantly asserted that Rome, and indeed the world, would for its sins be consumed by fire, and doubtless some had been heard during the progress of the conflagration declaring — as fanatics declared at the great fires in London and in Chicago — that the end of the world had come in accordance with their predictions. More than all, the Christians were friendless. If the calm and judicial Tacitus could consider them "a sort of people who held a new and impure superstition," and call their faith "a deadly fanaticism;" if Suetonius could describe them as "a people always making disturbances at the instigation of one Chrestus;" if the amiable Pliny could label Christianity "a depraved, wicked, and fatal superstition," it requires little imagination to conceive how the base and ignorant rabble regarded the followers of Christ.

Nero felt safe in declaring that the Christians had fired Rome. To emphasize the accusation he condemned them all to death. The gates of the city were watched to prevent their escape. To gratify his own delight in cruelty and at the same time please the populace, the emperor arranged the executions in the form of a public entertainment.

The horror of this spectacle was unprecedented. "There followed," says Uhlhorn, "a carnival of bloodshed such as Rome, thoroughly accustomed as it then was to murder, had never yet seen. It was not enough simply to put the supposed criminals to death, for of course the more cruelly they were treated, the more guilty they would be made to appear. And so the most horrible torments were employed, and new modes of execution were invented to torture them. Those who were crucified and thus imitated their Lord in their death could consider themselves favored. Others were sewn up in the skins of wild beasts and torn to pieces by dogs. Still others were used in tragic spectacles in the manner before mentioned." (The allusion is to executions in which the condemned were compelled to enact classic tragedies of Greece with absolute reality; in which "Hercules ascended on his funeral pyre and was burned alive, with complete theatrical machinery for the delight of a sight loving people.") In this Neronic persecution, continues Uhlhorn, "Christian women personating the Danaids and Dirce were brought upon the stage, and there certainly happened to the one who represented Dirce, what, according to the legend befell her, namely, that she was bound to a raging bull, and dragged to death."

At night-fall the imperial gardens were opened to the public. They were brilliantly illuminated. Huge torches lined the avenues, reddening the ponds and making the fountains jets of crimson. Each torch was a Christian wound in tow saturated with pitch and touched with fire. By this light Nero attired as a charioteer, drove his golden chariot along the winding ways.

But Nero overreached himself. He intended to increase the popular detestation of the Christians. He greatly diminished it. The atrocities inflicted upon them so greatly exceeded any cruelties ever seen in Rome before that even the Romans felt a reaction of pity. They began in some slight degree to sympathize with the despised sect. Its numbers increased. The fact is significant. The sight of torture in the arena endured as pagans endured it had made the Romans brutes. The sight of torture in the same arena endured as Christians endured it was among the most effective means by which those brutes were reformed into men. The centurion had probably witnessed many a crucifixion, and been hardened by every one he had seen, when the crucifixion of Christ moved him to exclaim, "This man was the Son of God." It is said that the frequent sight of suffering blunts the sympathies. The truth of the saying is proved by the experiences of some nurses and of some physicians. But the sight of suffering endured as Christ endured it tends to make men tender. And that fact, confirmed in many a hospital, is proved by the conversion of the Roman Empire. This is the truth which underlies the familiar proverb, "The blood of the martyrs is the seed of the church."

The persecution by Nero was not confined to Rome. Asia Minor felt its fury. But it was not general throughout the empire. It was a sudden outburst of passionate malignity caused by the crime and cowardice of a single man.

Before it had ceased Nero erected upon land cleared by the great fire a palace which has probably never been equaled in costliness and size. The grounds were magnificently adorned. "Expansive lakes," says Tacitus, "and fields of vast extent were intermixed with pleasing variety. Woods and forests stretched to an immeasurable length, presenting gloom and solitude amid scenes of open space, where the eye wandered with delight over an unbounded prospect." One of these lakes, Suetonius declares, was "like a sea." It occupied the site on which the Colosseum stands, and was the favorite place for gladiatorial sea-fights. The palace was included in triple porticoes a mile in length.

The baths were supplied with fresh water by a special aqueduct from Alba, with sea water by a second aqueduct from Ostia, and the hot mineral springs of Tivoli, eighteen miles away, were made to empty into them.

Some of the banqueting rooms were paneled and ceiled with mother-of-pearl, others with ivory, and others still were inclosed in walls of translucent alabaster. The walls and ceiling of one apartment were faced throughout with plates of solid gold thickly studded with pearls and precious stones. From concealed openings flowers were strewn and precious unguents dropped like dew upon the banqueters. The principal feasting hall was underneath a spacious dome, which revolved, by means of noiseless machinery, day and night, like the sky. A passage in Varro's "Res Rustica" makes it probable that the time of day was continuously shown by the changing positions of stars set in the revolving hemisphere, and it is certain that there was some connection between the succession of courses at the banquet and the movement of the ceiling.

A statue of Nero in gilded bronze, one hundred and twenty feet high, stood in the portico before the palace, and a portrait of the same criminal in still larger size was painted upon the wall behind the statue.

Within this "Golden House" the loathsome creature who had built it spent the days in nameless orgies. Among the least execrable of his crimes against nature were the assassination of his mother, and the brutal murder of his wife. At night he sallied forth to outrage and pillage his subjects in the streets of the city, followed by a band of gladiators to protect him from any who resisted his infamous assaults.

I. While this delirium of cruelty, extravagance and shame raged at Rome, the awful occurrences which preceded the destruction of Jerusalem began to multiply in the East.

The Jews had already drawn upon themselves an almost universal detestation. The heathen felt toward them as some of the United States feel in our time toward the Chinese. For the Jews went everywhere, but became nowhere citizens. They grew rich, were exempt from military service, contributed an infinitesimal amount to the taxes under which the rest of the empire groaned, took no interest in the state or its affairs, and regarded all Gentiles with aversion and contempt. They had earned for themselves the title inherited from them by the Christians, " Enemies of the human race."

A fresh rebellion broke out in Jerusalem. The Romans, advancing to suppress it, sacked Cæsarea with great slaughter. The Gentiles of Alexandria assembled to send to Nero an assurance of their loyalty. Before the ensuing tumults ended, they had emphasized those assurances by the massacre of fifty thousand Jewish citizens. At Damascus they proved their devotion to Rome by murdering ten thousand more. Wherever the reports of these outrages spread, the Gentiles rejoiced to hear of them, and the Gentiles had not yet learned to distinguish between Christians and Jews. Meantime, Nero, the monstrous head of this anarchy of horror, was traversing Greece, singing like a circus clown in competition for prizes at the public games.

The war which terminated in the siege of Jerusalem, by Titus, virtually began with the massacre at Cæsarea. The horrors of that siege are unparalleled in history. More than a million Jews were slaughtered or starved, and of the temple not one stone was left upon another. No Christian perished in the siege, for all Christians had left the city before it began. But the destruction of the Holy City was scarcely less a shock to Christians than to Jews. Nero, it is true, was dead when the temple fell, but the belief prevailed throughout the East that he was still alive, concealed in Parthia, and would soon return to repeat with exaggerated fury his blasphemies and persecutions. James, Peter, and Paul had all been killed. Of the great apostles, those counted pillars in the church, John alone survived.

At this crisis of horror and consternation — a crisis never paralleled in the history of the church — when the end of all things seemed near, and the eyes of Christians could discern only reasons for dismay; when other disciples saw their hopes buried beneath the falling walls of the old Jerusalem, and heard only the shrieks of the tortured, and the groans of the dying, the disciple whom Jesus loved discerned amid the universal ruin, "The Holy City, New Jerusalem, coming down from God, out of heaven, adorned as a bride for her husband;" heard above the shrieks of pain and the wail of despair "a new song, and harpers harping with their harps." In the sea of carnage he saw a great white throne, unshaken, immovable, rising high above the puny rage of Nero, and in the midst of the throne a lamb, as it had been slain. Looking upward from the torches in Nero's gardens, and the forest of crosses there, from the bodies of mangled saints, and destroying beasts, he saw radiant creatures standing near the throne, whom He that sat thereon was not ashamed to call his brethren, and heard a voice which said, "These are they which come out of the great tribulation."

This is the genesis of that noblest and most inspiring of Christian poems, the Apocalypse. It has been in times of affliction the stay of the church. If men use it as the triumphal hymn of the ages, as St. Bernard used it; as the slaves on Southern rice fields used it, when the crack of the overseer's whip was drowned in the songs of the New Jerusalem; as we have often used it when, amid the wrecks of shattered households, we point from the ruined corse to the throne that cannot be ruined; if we use it thus, as the inspired assurance that every wrong shall die, and every right shall triumph, that love is immortal, that every tear shall be wiped away, and that they who trust the Saviour cannot die ; then the Apocalypse, the Rent Vail, will prove to us also the whisper of God, the breath of Paradise, bringing spring upon the winter of this world. If we turn to the book, expecting to find in it some key that will unlock the future, and betray to a faithless curiosity the secrets of God, it will drive us, if we are earnest men, as it has driven many such before us, towards insanity or atheism.

Given, as we have seen, through the inspirations of the first persecution, the Apocalypse remained the support of the church in sharper and more ghastly persecutions which were to come.

II. At the close of the first century the Christians were still considered Jews. The world regarded them as a Jewish sect like the Pharisees, the Sadducees, the Essenes, the Herodians, or the Zealots. Early in the second century they began to be recognized as a distinct and separate people. The Roman government discerned instinctively in the church an irreconcilable antagonist. An antagonist respectful, obedient to law, never resisting violence, nor returning evil for evil, soft as velvet, but firm as steel. The church affected the pagan world as a pure wife clothed in the invincible strength of gentleness affects a vicious and brutal husband. The husband must mend his ways or be rid of his wife. Mankind must obey Christ or crucify Him. The Roman government recognized the fact it could not explain. It or Christianity must perish. The duel began by the attempt to compel Christians to worship Cæsar, and reached its climax in the reign of Decius and Valerian.

At the beginning of the second century, Trajan had pronounced Christianity unlawful. But he had taken pains to prevent the enforcement of his own decree. The later persecutions were intended to exterminate Christianity. The whole power of the government with its multitudinous ramifications reaching from the Euphrates to the Tagus was exerted to achieve that end.

One of the most authentic and thrilling narratives of the martyrdoms is that of Polycarp at Smyrna. He was born before the destruction of Jerusalem, had been a disciple of John, and had doubtless often heard from the lips of the disciple whom Jesus loved the truths we read in his Gospel, and the hopes we gather from his vision. Therefore it is not strange that when the crowd clamored for the blood of Polycarp the proconsul was fascinated by his spirit, or that when the proconsul exclaimed, "Speak one word against Christ, and I can save you!" the old man answered, "Eighty and six years have I served Him, and He never did me wrong. How can I blaspheme my king who has saved me?"

They had brought him to the place of execution mounted upon an ass, I suppose to ridicule his Master. Once more the proconsul tried to save him: "If you will not revile Christ, swear by the Genius of the emperor!" "I am a Christian." "Then speak to the people, move them as you have moved me." "I owed you an answer, for we are told to honor the powers that be, but I owe them nothing but to love them." The wild beasts were shown him, the stake, the fagots. "Only do not bind me. He who strengthens me to endure the fire will not let me flinch."

As the flames curled round him and crisped the martyr's flesh, they heard the old man saying, "Lord God almighty, Father of our Lord Jesus Christ, I praise Thee that Thou hast judged me worthy of this day and of this hour, to share in the number of thy witnesses, and in the cup of thy Christ."

Though persecution was inexorably pressed, neither Christian nor pagan has recorded a single malediction uttered by its victims. The flames which burned them bore upward blessings upon their enemies and prayers for those who despitefully used and persecuted them. Men came to mock their agonies, and departed worshiping their Saviour. This legalized persecution also failed, and failed utterly. The number of Christians was larger at its close than at its beginning.

III. The last persecution was inspired mainly by religious motives. It was therefore the fiercest of all.

The Christians seemed to the heathens atheists, because they worshiped nothing visible, and not to worship an image appeared to the Roman world not to worship at all.

Diocletian was emperor. He was at once a statesman and a sincerely religious pagan. The son of a slave, he had risen to supreme power by his own abilities. While he was still in the ranks near Paris, a Druid priestess had told him he would become emperor when he had slain the boar. In vain he hunted the forests of Ardennes and slaughtered the wild swine there. But when he killed Aper, who was accused of assassinating Numerianus, the soldiers chose him emperor by acclamation, and it was remembered that *aper* means a boar.

Diocletian was long restrained from persecuting the Christians by his own sagacity. Near the close of his reign, when his powers had begun to fail, he was persuaded by his colleague, the fierce and stupid Galerius, to take the foolish step. The Christians in the eastern part of the empire are supposed to have numbered at that time about one in twelve of the population; in the western, about one in fifteen. But though so small a minority, they exceeded in number any one of the many pagan sects. They were massed in cities, while the pagans, as their name implies, were scattered through the country districts. In Antioch a single church contained fifty thousand members. Some of the highest offices in the empire were filled by Christians, and the empress herself was suspected of being one of them. More than all, the Christians were animated by a zeal which the heathen world could not match. These facts made persecution perilous. Despite the danger, the decree was issued. It was framed with great sagacity. Former attacks had been aimed at Christian men. This was aimed at Christian literature. It was sought to starve Christianity by destroying its food. Christians were not at first required to revile Christ or to worship Cæsar. They were only commanded to surrender their sacred books. All who possessed copies of any Christian writings were enjoined, on pain of death, to present them to be burned; all who knew where such writings were concealed were required to inform or suffer the same penalty. Imperial spies, stimulated by hope of large rewards, searched the empire. Inhuman tortures were applied to compel confession. Christians who surrendered their books were called *traditores*, or " givers up," and thus was coined that word of odious meaning, shortened at last into " traitor," which signifies a Christian who surrendered his books.

The persecution prompted by pagan passion failed, as we have seen, by exciting pity in the persecutors. The persecution inaugurated by pagan policy failed even more conspicuously and absolutely, and convinced Roman statesmen that Christian character and influence were essential to the welfare of the state. The persecution instituted by pagan piety under Diocletian ended in a still more striking reversal of the purpose it was intended to achieve. The 23d of February, 303, that persecution began. It was brought about and enforced by Galerius, and permitted by Diocletian in order to vindicate the honor of the pagan gods. It continued until 311. That year Galerius lay dying of a loathsome malady. Every pagan deity had been besought with fervent devotion for his restoration to health. Costly rites had been performed. Still the emperor grew worse. Then came a proclamation from his sick-chamber, dictated by himself. It granted liberty of worship to all Christians in the empire, and entreated them to pray for the emperor. In less than ten years the cross was emblazoned upon the arms of Constantine, and within fourteen Christianity had become the religion of the state.

The fact of surpassing interest about this last and most terrible of all the persecutions endured by the church is this. It gave us the New Testament. Planned to destroy the oracles of our faith, it only purified them. Those writings which Christians did not supremely value were surrendered, and burned.

Those which Christians counted more precious than life they preserved. Yielding the chaff, they kept the wheat. The canon of the New Testament was not formed by the decree of any man or body of men. It is simply those writings out of an enormous mass of early Christian literature which seemed to Christians so unspeakably precious that they risked their lives to save them.

The history of these persecutions is mournful but glorious. It records the triumph of Christ over the world, the flesh, and the devil, and reveals the foundations of the New Jerusalem laid in cement of blood.

XV.

NEW JERUSALEM, THE KING.

II.

MORE than eighteen hundred years ago there was in Palestine a workingman, a carpenter. He belonged to a humble family and lived in a small village which bore an evil reputation among its neighbors. Early in his life his mother became a widow, and until past his thirtieth year he worked at the bench, earning wages to support her. Then, when younger brothers could take his place at home, he laid down the plane and saw and began to preach. He said that his preaching was the Gospel of Almighty God. At times his kinsmen said he was beside himself, and once his mother seems to have thought him mad. In less than three years he had provoked so much hostility from the religious, which were the ruling classes of his countrymen, that they determined to kill him. They arrested him by treachery, tried him by perjury, and condemned him to death illegally upon the charge of blasphemy. That charge could not stand in a Roman court, as the Romans did not consider blasphemy, unless it was aimed at Cæsar, a capital offense. The Jews were subject to the laws of Rome. It was therefore necessary to convict the prisoner upon some other indictment. He was accused of sedition and arraigned before Pontius Pilate, a Roman official of Tiberius Cæsar. Acquitted by Pilate of every charge brought against him, he was nevertheless by Pilate's permission executed, in defiance of law, to please the Jews. During his trial and execution, which were exceptionally painful, the prisoner manifested rare fortitude, and, although he offered no resistance, quietly asserted that he was a king and would sometime be recognized and revered as such. He had been followed to Pilate's judgment hall by a furious mob clamoring for his death. He calmly insisted that he was their king.

The Roman soldiers, to whom the prisoner was a stranger, and who cannot therefore be supposed to have been prejudiced against him, treated his assertion with boisterous ridicule. They also appear to have considered him insane. They flung over him a robe of some coarse material, and of a color which grotesquely suggested the imperial scarlet. They plucked twigs from the hedges of white-thorn in Pilate's gardens, twisted them into a crown, and placed it on his head. They broke off a reed and thrust it as a sceptre between his palms, which were bound together, and knelt before him in coarse and brutal but jovial mockery. Soldiers in garrison with little to occupy their minds will often act like frolicsome children. So I have seen school-boys gather around a woman whose disordered brain mistook her rags for royal apparel, her tattered hood for a crown, and provoke her to yet crazier conduct by simulating reverence. It is almost an instinct of human nature to deride assumptions which appear exorbitant. The same impulse which moved slave-holders to call their negroes Scipio, Cato, and Cæsar, influenced the Roman soldiers to mock their prisoner. Even to those who knew and loved him, his claims appeared baseless, for they all forsook him and fled, though he had promised those who followed him to the end thrones beside his own.

When they had mocked and scourged him the soldiers led their victim to a place called Golgotha. There they nailed him to a wooden cross. Over it was written in three languages, that all might appreciate the irony, " Jesus of Nazareth, king of the Jews." For the prisoner's name was Jesus, he had lived at Nazareth, and he claimed to be king of the Jews.

After hanging upon the cross six hours he was supposed to be dead. It is even said that one of the soldiers thrust a spear into his heart and so proved that he was dead. But I will not insist upon that statement, because it has been doubted, and I would avoid any assertion which the most skeptical will question. I will therefore only say that many have believed, and many still believe, that the spear pierced the heart of Jesus. That statement no one will deny.

During the whole of this experience the man who was crucified made no resistance, but calmly persisted that he was a king, that some of those standing by would discern his kingdom before they died, and that eventually every knee should bow before him and every tongue confess that he was Lord.

All this occurred in a remote and petty province of the Roman Empire. It attracted no attention at the time beyond the limits of that province. Of all the classic historians only one refers to it, and he, Tacitus, who belonged to the next generation, dismisses the occurrence in three lines of his voluminous history with an implied apology for mentioning an incident so trivial among affairs of serious importance.

So the carpenter died. He had preached less than three years. His family, at times at least, thought him insane. The influential classes of his countrymen branded him an imposter. The Roman soldiers laughed at his pretensions. He left not a line of writing. There was no press to diffuse a knowledge of his words or deeds. He had no recognized disciples save a few unlettered men with neither wealth nor influence. When in the presence of death he declared himself a king, Jerusalem gnashed her teeth and Rome grinned.

I. Three hundred years have passed. The capital of the world is moving from Rome to Constantinople. We are at Nice, in Asia Minor. The city quivers with excitement. Strangers are hourly arriving. They come from far and near. The great military roads, the arteries of the empire, with their relays of horses conveying government officials a hundred miles a day, have been put at the service of these strangers. Each has been brought from his home, and will be returned to it, at government expense, and while absent is an honored guest of royalty. They have come from all parts of the civilized world. Three hundred and eighteen of them, who appear distinguished above the others, are assembled in the great hall of the imperial palace. They have been chosen as the ablest and most influential men of three continents, and are called overseers of other men, or, in Greek, bishops. The floor of the hall is oblong, and the bishops are seated around it as spectators in an amphitheatre. At the centre stands a low altar. On it lies a roll of closely written parchment. It is believed to contain reports of the words spoken and the deeds done three hundred years ago by the man who was crucified at Golgotha.

At a signal the august assembly rises. Every eye is strained toward the extremity of the apartment opposite the scroll. The wide doors open. A stately figure enters the hall alone. He is almost a giant in stature and in strength. But his form is symmetrical and very beautiful. His face is ruddy like the face of a Saxon. His eyes are deep blue, and his long fair hair falls in thick masses about his shoulders. He is counted the kingliest looking man of his time. Upon his forehead rests the imperial diadem of pearls. His helmet has been laid aside, or the cross would appear above the eagle. His mantle of imperial scarlet blazes with jewels. This man is Constantine, the successor of Pilate's master. Reverently and unattended, he advances towards the scroll and bends before it. A throne of carved wood adorned with gold has been placed for him. He will not be seated until one of the three hundred, representing the rest, commands him to take his throne in the name of the man who was crucified at Golgotha.

There are hundreds of officials, each the peer of Pilate. A word of Constantine will send them all to death without appeal, and Constantine addresses the representatives of the Nazarene whom Pilate's soldiers mocked as "My fathers," and tells them he has brought them together that they may teach him how to worship most acceptably the man who was crucified at Golgotha. Three hundred years ago the rabble at Jerusalem were shouting, "Away with him! We will have no king but Cæsar!" Now Cæsar answers back, "I have no king but Christ."

II. Sixty-five years more have passed. The emperor Theodosius has come to Milan to offer thanks and prayers to the Giver of victories in the city of the venerated Ambrose. Attended by military guards and courtiers, he approaches the church. His foot is lifted to ascend its steps. A priest holding a crucifix before him stands in the porch, and forbids the monarch's further advance. It is Ambrose. In the name of Christ he reminds his sovereign of the massacre at Thessalonica, and declares that no unrepentant murderer shall enter the holy place, though that murderer be Cæsar. The emperor humbly remonstrates: "David committed homicide, and David was forgiven." "As you have imitated David in his crimes, imitate David in his repentance." And the master of the Roman Empire suffers himself to be stripped of the insignia of royalty, to be clothed in sackcloth, and after eight months of penance he will be thankful for permission to enter the church, where, prostrate upon the marble pavement, he will entreat with sighs and tears forgiveness from the man who was crucified at Golgotha.

III. Other centuries have passed. The Empire has perished. Cæsar is a tradition, Rome a ruin. A new power has arisen in the West. The kingdom of the Franks has come. Charlemagne is now the foremost man in the world. He has conquered most of Europe. He has subdued Italy, and now is worshiping at Rome because, the fathers tell him, it is the day on which angels sang over the birth of his king at Bethlehem; the last Christmas day of the eighth century. While he kneels in the Cathedral of St. Peter ignorant, he will afterwards declare, of what is coming to himself, and absorbed in the solemnities of devotion, the Pope approaches him from behind and crowns him emperor of the Holy Roman Empire, in the name of the man who was crucified at Golgotha.

Twenty-six years before, the monarch had assumed at Monza the Lombard crown, which made him virtually sovereign of Italy. It is, perhaps, impossible to say with certainty whether the existing Lombard crown is identical with that which was used by Charlemagne, or a reproduction made in the thirteenth century. Neither is it important to our purpose to decide. It is sufficient to know that it has generally been believed to be the same, and that those who have worn it, Charles V. and Napoleon among them, have assumed it to be the iron crown which was used in the coronation of Lombard kings from the days of Queen Theodelinda and which rested upon the brow of Charlemagne.

It is the most celebrated diadem in the world, and has been more revered than all others combined. It is a circle of broad gold plates so joined as to form a ribbon-like band, adorned with blue enamel, embossed with flowers, and set with a few large sapphires, rubies, and emeralds. Neither the gold, nor the gems, nor the workmanship have given it the unique reverence which it still retains. Within the golden circle runs a thin rim of iron. Millions have believed that it was made from one of the nails that pierced the feet of the man who was crucified at Golgotha. Without contending for the truth of the tradition, it is certain that, partly because of it, in the course of twelve hundred years some of the most powerful monarchs in the world have sought to increase their glory by placing this crown upon their heads; and that Napoleon, when near the pinnacle of his greatness, established the order which, afterwards adopted by Francis of Austria, took rank among the most honorable in Europe, the Order of the Iron Crown.

No single incident in history, it seems to me, illustrates more suggestively the contrast between real and apparent power, than that which occurred in the great Cathedral of Milan on the 26th of May, 1805, when Napoleon, the ablest monarch who has lived for eighteen centuries, surrounded by an apparently invincible army of soldiers who adored him, and watched by a world that feared him; grasping the strongest sword ever intrusted to a human hand, took the iron crown with the words: "God has given it to me; let him touch it who dares!" and crowned himself with one of the nails which had pierced the Galilean's foot. In a few years the man who closed his hand to clutch the sword plunged from Tilsit to St. Helena. The man who opened his hand to receive the nails still continues his triumphant march above the slopes of Calvary up the everlasting hills.

IV. Other centuries have passed. Charlemagne is buried in romance. Europe has been roused from a long torpor. An enthusiasm never paralleled at any other period of her history has swept her people. It has thrilled from London to Vienna, from Paris to Prague. It has fired the monarch on his throne and the peasant in his hovel. Before it ends kings, courtiers, artisans, women, and little children will be rushing towards the Orient. Monarchs have mortgaged their whole revenues, nobles have sold all their possessions to purchase equipments of war. The interest felt to-day in questions of capital and labor is a calm stream compared to the passion which agitated Europe in the eleventh century. What was the object to win which those men counted power, wealth, and life itself cheaply given? They were minded to rescue from sacrilegious hands the spot of earth where they believed that once for three days had lain the dead body of the man who was crucified at Golgotha.

The crusaders have penetrated Asia. They have captured Antioch. But the Saracens have come in countless numbers. The Christian army has been beaten back within the defenses of the city and is besieged within its walls. Famine and disease have begun their work. The champions of the cross are dispirited. They sue for mercy. It is haughtily refused. Their leaders strive in vain to make them sally. Repulsed so often, they cannot be persuaded to renew the battle. Cowed, despairing, they await within the walls the death which seems inevitable and near.

So was it at sunset. The next sunrise found the streets of Antioch ringing with triumphant battle-hymns sung by soldiers eager to be led against the enemy. The ardor of the Christian army was with difficulty restrained until the festival of St. Paul and St. Peter. On that day the city gates were flung fearlessly open. The walls were thronged by women and children quivering with the excitement of anticipated victory. A company of monks marched forth, chanting, "Let the Lord God arise, let his enemies be scattered." They were led by Raymond d'Agiles. He bore in his hands as a standard a spear shaft surmounted by a rusted barb. In twelve battalions, each named after one of the apostles, the crusading army followed. They advanced toward the besieging army. The Saracens could not believe their eyes. But they could not withstand the charge. Led by the iron standard, the Christians were irresistible. At night-fall the Saracens had vanished, all of them but 100,000 corpses said to have been left upon the field.

What made these cowed men brave? Not the refreshment of sleep, for they had spent the night in a vigil of prayer! Not the strength of food, for famine stalked the streets of Antioch! They believed that in answer to their supplications their leaders had found beneath the pavement of the Cathedral, and that Raymond bore before their eyes, the spear which had pierced the heart of the man who was crucified at Golgotha. In the flakes of rust upon it they recognized stains of the "blood shed for many," and that conviction made them irresistible.

V. Still the years pass. We are at Paris. It is the 18th of July, 1239 A. D. Eight days ago the king with the royal family, the court, and the highest dignitaries of the church, rode forth upon the road to Troyes. They rode silently as men filled with solemn recollections. At Villeneuve, five miles from Sens, they met another procession reverently guarding what appeared to be a chest of treasure. At sight of it the royal cavalcade dismounted. The monarch, with the royal family and the archbishop, was permitted to approach and view the treasure. It had been brought from Constantinople. When rumors of its removal were whispered in the East, the king of Greece instantly dispatched the swiftest ships in his navy to intercept and take possession of the prize. The captain commanding the vessel that bore it refused a military escort, convinced that Heaven would protect a freight so holy, and the counselors at Constantinople agreed in his opinion. It reached Venice safely, and there was guarded at the Cathedral of St. Mark as the most valuable object in the city. The emperor of Germany gave safe and honorable conduct to those transporting it to France. Thus Constantinople, Greece, Italy, Germany, and France, each in a different way, expressed their appreciation of its value, and those who carried it added their testimony that Heaven watched over its safety, since no rain fell during their journey except at night when the treasure was protected, and rain was needed to lay the dust which might otherwise defile it on the morrow.

The royal family knelt around the wooden coffer. They gazed long upon its contents, rained their tears upon it, and gave thanks to God. The next day the king returned to Paris to prepare for its reception there. Eight days were consumed in the preparations. The great day arrived. The shops were closed. The streets were thronged. From the Faubourg St. Antoine to the Cathedral of Notre Dame they were carpeted, and the buildings adjacent hung with costly tapestries. The entire court, with the queen and the royal ladies, followed by a vast procession, moved toward the Cathedral. In the van was every ecclesiastic of Paris. All marched on foot. Between the churchmen and the court walked the king and his oldest brother, the duke of Artois. Both were barefooted, and clad only in coarse woolen shirts. Upon their shoulders they bore the precious treasure. The people, we may believe, knelt and crossed themselves as it pssed by, and only the tolling of bells was heard in the silent city.

Before the procession entered Paris the treasure it escorted had been displayed to the people. A throne was placed upon a platform in the suburb of St. Antoine.

Around it, upon the platform, knelt the most illustrious men of France. Beyond the platform a countless multitude waited upon the ground. All eyes were fixed upon him as the archbishop lifted the wooden lid and took from beneath it a silver casket marked with the seals of Constantinople and Venice. From the silver casket the same hands took a smaller one of gold. From this the archbishop lifted, and, before placing it upon the throne, held aloft in view of the awe-struck worshipers a chaplet of withered thorns! They were believed to be those which, plucked by mocking soldiers from the hedges of Pilate's gardens, had pierced the brow of the man who was crucified at Golgotha.

Therefore France paid for them a sum which saved the Eastern Empire from bankruptcy, and therefore when they were laid in the most holy chapel of Paris which the king built to receive them and other memorials of the Galilean, the city felt secured from all evil by the blessing of God.

You have stood at Rome in the great cathedral. In the broad aisle beneath its sky-like dome stately churches might stand in triple rank with unbent spires. Have you looked upon that miracle of architecture without reflecting, "All that is noblest in art and most fertile in genius have here combined to perpetuate the memory of Simon Peter, only because he served the man whom a Jewish menial jeered him for knowing, the man who was crucified at Golgotha."

In the same city is a marble stairway. Each step is deeply worn by the knees of those who have ascended it. Less than thirty years ago, I have been told, a queen and a beggar might have been seen upon it side by side. Neither seemed conscious of the other's presence. They moved slowly, upon their knees, pausing on every step to pray. They believed that once, down those same steps from Pilate's judgment hall, dropping blood as he went, had walked the man who was crucified at Golgotha. "At the name of Jesus every knee shall bow."

You have visited the Campo Santo at Pisa? There, inclosed in marble colonnades which artists still make pilgrimages to admire, lie the bones of some of the best and noblest of Italy. They craved interment there as the richest boon posterity could give them, because they believed that the dust brought from Palestine might once have been pressed by the feet of the man who was crucified at Golgotha.

But these are idle superstitions, the thistle-down of history! They are so, and therefore I repeat them. Thistle-down may show how the aerial currents move when boulders give no signs. A superstition is a fact as truly as Gibraltar, and facts are to be accounted for. How shall we account for these? Why were such honors never paid to any other man? To-day Jesus Christ is the central fact of human history. No man offers a system of philosophy without feeling that he must in some way explain the obvious position and apparent influence of Jesus Christ. Those who do not love him recognize his presence. Those who do not confess him king, still must classify themselves by the relation they sustain toward him; for he is the Greenwich whence the longitudes of time are calculated, the sun which tells us in what latitude we sail. Gibbon, the ablest historian, I think, who has ever lived, hating Christianity and eager to abolish faith in its founder, writes his Decline and Fall of the Roman Empire. But Gibbon, equally with the most ardent Christian, must confess the sovereignty of Christ by writing every date, not A. U. C., from the founding of Rome, but A. D., from the year of Our Lord, before men will understand or read or buy his book.

Napoleon reminded Bertrand that no man had ever lived for whom a century after his death a single individual could be found willing to die, though after eighteen centuries millions would gladly give their lives for Jesus Christ. "I know men," said the emperor "and Jesus Christ is not a man." Shall we venture to class him with Socrates and Confucius? Why do ladies choose to wear upon their bosoms crosses of gold or pearls or diamonds? Why have they not taught jewelers to carve them cups of malachite or emerald for ornaments to commemorate the death of Socrates? The cross was the symbol of uttermost degradation and ignominy, the gibbet of the ancient world, until some power lifted it from the mire and stamped it upon the sky in stars. One cannot visit the opera, the theatre, or any place of fashion without seeing on every hand in letters of living light the sign of the Son of man, and reading if one has eyes that see, " To him every knee shall bow."

That Jesus did not rise from the dead, and that he wrought no miracles may be safely conceded to any man who will without the resurrection and without the miracles adequately explain the place held by Jesus Christ to-day. By denying the miracles we only make miracles of the conceded facts. Before us stands a column overtopping by an immeasurable altitude every other pedestal on earth. No stairway winds around it. No ladder made by hands has ever reached so high. Upon it stands the man we once saw sitting by the well, wearied with his journey. How did he get there? We are told he has no wings. Miracles are only wings which help us to explain the facts we are impotent to deny.

There are parts of the earth which we justly call benighted. They are the parts of it which have not yet learned to worship Christ. All that are potent among nations we clasp in one great word and call Christendom or Christ's Kingdom.

Whatever is ennobling in art, stable in statesmanship, uplifting in social life, has grown out of the Galilean's grave. To name a thought, a word, a deed " unchristian " is to brand it with a stamp of infamy. Free labor was scarcely known upon the earth, and slaves were the only workingmen outside of Palestine when Jesus died a slave's death at Golgotha. How many are the slaves in Christendom to-day, and at whose command have the fetters been broken? Wherever Jesus Christ is trusted and obeyed, sin and sorrow flee away. How shall we account for these facts? Can we be saved by lies?

We have watched the careers of other conquerors. Has Christ gained the crown which grows more radiant each century as they have won the crowns which crumble with the years?

Cast your cannon of a hundred tons. Load it to the muzzle. Tip your shot with pointed steel. Apply the spark, and you can send your bolt 1,200 feet a second. In that second, light flashes 200,000 miles. "That," says Victor Hugo, "is the difference between Napoleon Bonaparte and Jesus Christ." We think it only a part of the difference. The whole appears to us to be that Christ was Napoleon's creator.

www.ingramcontent.com/pod-product-compliance
Lightning Source LLC
Chambersburg PA
CBHW022112230426
43672CB00008B/1360